FONTANA BRITISH BATTLEFIELDS

This series forms a unique handbook to the major battles fought on English and Scottish soil from Arthur's victory at Mount Badon in AD 516 to the butchery of Cumberland at Culloden in 1746. As guides to the sites and as exercises in historical reconstruction, these books will fascinate local historians, readers of all things military, walkers, and tourists alike.

The books not only explain why particular battles were fought and what the human, military, and historical consequences were, but also give accurate details of where the battlefields are, how they can be found, and what to look for. Thus armed, the visitor can walk the battlefield himself, following the account of the battle, and see at first-hand how decisive the elements and topography have been in British history.

In the preparation for this series Philip Warner, Senior Lecturer at the Royal Military Academy, Sandhurst, has not only read all the surviving first-hand accounts, but has walked every battlefield himself.

Also available

The S....

D0530820

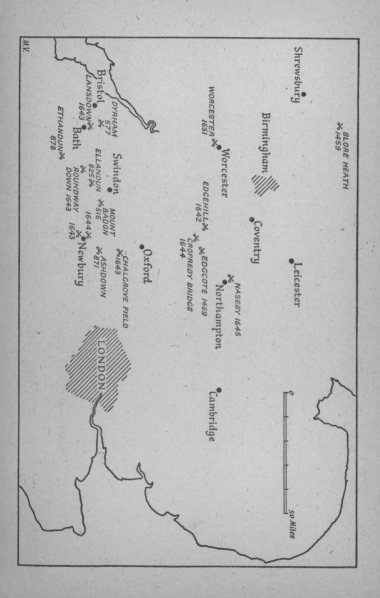

M.V.

Shrewsbury •

BLORE HEATH
✗ 1459

Birmingham •

DYRHAM
577 ✗
Bristol •
LANSDOWN
1643 ✗
Bath •
ETHANDUN ✗
878

WORCESTER ✗
1651

Worcester •

Swindon •
ELLANDUN
825 ✗
MOUNT
BADON
✗ 516
ROUNDWAY
DOWN 1643 ✗
Newbury •
ASHDOWN
✗ 871

EDGEHILL ✗
1642

CROPREDY BRIDGE
1644
✗ EDGCOTE 1469

Coventry •

NASEBY 1645
✗
Northampton •

Leicester •

Oxford •
CHALGROVE FIELD
✗ 1643

LONDON

Cambridge •

0

50 Miles

Philip Warner

FAMOUS BATTLES OF THE MIDLANDS

Where battles were fought
Why they were fought
How they were won and lost

Fontana/Collins

First published in Great Britain under the title
British Battlefields: The Midlands by
Osprey Publishing Ltd 1973
First issued in Fontana 1976

The maps in this book are based on the Ordnance Survey
map with the sanction of the Controller of H.M. Stationery
Office, Crown Copyright Reserved

Made and printed in Great Britain by
William Collins Sons & Co. Ltd Glasgow

Contents

List of Maps

I Mount Badon: **O.S. Map First Series no. 174 (158), grid reference 282 778.** This takes you to Baydon village as you follow the Roman road (Ermine Street) on the Newbury-Wickham-Baydon line. Baydon is the highest village in Wiltshire. If you continue west up the road from Baydon village this will take you to the Ridgeway crossing, and on your left you will see Liddington Hill fort (209 799).

II Dyrham (Deorham): **O.S. Map First Series no. 172 (156), grid reference 740 769.** This is very close to the A46-B4465 crossroads.

III Ellandun: **O.S. Map First Series no. 173 (157), grid reference 085 655.** Take the A4 from Marlborough to Overton (or West Kennet) and walk up the Wansdyke. This will take you through the battlefield.

IV Ashdown: **O.S. Map First Series no. 158 (158), grid reference 542 817.** Take the A417 from Streatley and turn left just as it leaves the village at the sign marked 'To the Golf Club'. The road goes past the club and becomes the track leading to the Ridgeway. Bear right towards Lowbury Hill.

V Ethandun: **O.S. Map First Series no. 184 (167), grid reference 925 525.** Take the B3098 to Edington. The ambush position is along the side of the hill.

VI Blore Heath: **O.S. Map First Series no. 127 (119), grid reference 713 353.** Take the A53 out of Market Drayton; the battlefield will be found on the right of this road after three

miles. Permission must be obtained from Audley's Cross
Farm to view the site.

VII Edgcote: **O.S. Map First Series no. 151 (145), grid
reference 515 466.** Take the A422 out of Banbury, and take
the farm track on the left past Lower Thorpe. This will bring
you on to Danes Moor. Alternatively it may be approached
via the B4036, turning right at Wardington to reach Edgcote
Lodge.

VIII Edgehill: **O.S. Map First Series no. 151 (145), grid
reference 357 492.** This is a convenient battlefield to find
but difficult to inspect closely. Readers will find it easier to
make the circuit of the battlefield.

IX Chalgrove Field: **O.S. Map First Series no. 165 (139),
grid reference 644 972.** Chalgrove is on the B480. Take the
Warpsgrove road out of Chalgrove; this will lead you past
the Hampden monument which marks the battlefield.

X Lansdown: **O.S. Map First Series no. 172 (156), grid
reference 725 705.** The A46 Bath-Stroud runs through the
middle of the battlefield area but take the A420 to Tog Hill.
Turn left to Freezing Hill and continue to the Granville
Memorial on the edge of Lansdown Hill.

XI Roundway Down: **O.S. Map First Series no. 173 (157),
grid reference 015 655.** It is possible to walk around and
over most of this battlefield which probably varies little from
the day on which it was fought over.

XII First Newbury: **O.S. Map First Series no. 174 (158),
grid reference 455 653.** Take the A343 out of Newbury and
turn right at the Gun Inn. Although built up, the battlefield
is clearly discernible.

XIII Cropredy Bridge: **O.S. Map First Series no. 151 (145),**

grid reference 472 466. The approach march and battle may be followed by taking the A423 from Banbury and turning off by Great Bourton.

XIV Second Newbury: **O.S. Map First Series no. 174 (158), grid reference 465 685.** This battlefield is very easily found by taking the A34 out of Newbury and turning off for Donnington Castle.

XV Naseby: **O.S. Map First Series no. 141 (133), grid reference 681 799.** The Naseby-Sibbertoft road runs right through the battlefield. The monument is on the west of this road. The obelisk just outside Naseby village on the B4036 is unfortunately misleading as it is well away from the battlefield.

XVI Worcester: **O.S. Map First Series no. 150 (143), grid reference 845 525.** This gives the first phase of the contest. Red Hill may be traced along the A422 in Worcester.

Note on Map References

All ordnance survey maps are overlaid with an arrangement of numbered lines called the grid system, which enables any point on a map to be easily and accurately identified.

A map reference is given in two sets of three figures, for example 396 112. The first two figures of each trio (39 and 11) are the vertical line (northings) and the horizontal line (eastings) respectively; they intersect in the south-west (bottom left) corner of the square to which they refer. Smaller divisions of the square are not marked but may be estimated, and the third figures of each trio (6 and 2) represent the 'tenths' of the lines east and north (right and upwards). Thus 396 112 indicates a point six-tenths east and two-tenths north of the intersection of northing 39 and easting 11.

As the side of a square represents one kilometre (1000 metres) a tenth of that line must represent 100 metres: thus map references are correct to 100 metres.

The first map number given refers in each case to the 1 : 50 000 series. This replaced the old one inch to one mile series (the number given in brackets) in 1974. However, the maps reproduced are from the one inch to one mile series.

Introduction

For the man who is interested in warfare and who likes to walk the ground, deducing how battles were lost and won, there is no more fascinating study than the early battlefields. Here his theories will be as valid as those of any historian, military or otherwise, and he may well have a flash of insight that will solve a mystery which has lasted for a thousand years. The early battlefields are often set in open countryside which has changed much less than the landscape elsewhere; this makes his task easier. He will be advised to equip himself with a $2\frac{1}{2}$-inch map, a prismatic compass, and perhaps a pair of binoculars. The binoculars will save his legs, and perhaps more if he uses them to inspect herds of cows. I have encountered more than one farm where a bull was loose in a field with a footpath running through it!

Battles and battlefields throw much light on history at any period but the interest of the early battles is that small bodies of men fighting with primitive weapons often determined the shape and composition of future nations. At Hastings approximately 9000 Normans changed the course of history; in earlier battles smaller numbers had accomplished nearly as much.

To understand the early battles it is necessary to see oneself as a member of one side or the other; it does not matter whether as victor or vanquished. Having taken sides you should approach the battlefield from the direction by which your own army approached. As you do so you should consider all alternative courses of action – apart from making a hasty retreat. Are you, as you move forward, sufficiently alert to the possibilities of surprise? As you ponder on your possible courses of action – and the enemy's – making, in fact, a military appreciation, that long-past situation will suddenly become almost embarrassingly real. You may perhaps experience that peculiar feeling, half apprehension, half excitement, that you are now on the most dangerous path you have ever trod. At the same time you may feel that this is destiny and that you would not wish it otherwise. You, for better or worse, are playing your part in great events. Once the battle has begun you will have no time for thoughts, speculative or otherwise. You will be driven by the needs of the moment, and whether you are alive at the end of the battle will depend on training, luck, and perhaps even your own skill at arms. Whatever happens, even if you come through without a scratch (which is unlikely), you will never be the same person again.

In considering battles, do not believe contemporary accounts without question. Some are entirely reliable but they are far outnumbered by those which are not. Few military despatches avoid bias of one sort or another, and when one compares the accounts of opposing sides in any battle it is often difficult to realize they are describing the same events and place. Minor successes are magnified; major setbacks glossed over. Sycophants were just as plentiful in former times as they are today. Critics of a successful and powerful person were however much less plentiful. Nowadays it is commonplace for people whose naval experience is limited to a Channel crossing to criticize the tactics at Trafalgar or Jutland, and other people of no military experience at all are apt to be very severe indeed with the Montgomeries, Slims, MacArthurs and Pattons; rather less was heard of such armchair strategists in medieval times. Not unwisely the valiant non-combatant preferred to wait till his subjects and their near relatives were dead before voicing his criticisms; he might otherwise have been offered practical opportunities to exercise his military knowledge.

It is widely known that once the first shot is fired, or the first blow struck, there descends on any battlefield 'the fog of war'. Orders are given, misinterpreted, misunderstood, delayed, even disobeyed. Confused and conflicting reports are sent back to commanders who are hard put to distinguish which side is which in the confused struggling mass ahead of and around them. Almost every report is alarmist or exaggerated. A few lucky hits by arrows or gunshot could throw a whole line into confusion and the actual ground might display all sorts of unexpected qualities. The Battle of Agincourt was partly won by the English bowmen but was more a matter of a battle lost to the French by treacherous mud than won by any great skill from their opponents. Unfortunately in the very early battles there is no record of the exact date on which they were fought. Undoubtedly they would have been in the summer months but the result in many turned perhaps on whether there were leaves on the trees, and whether the ground was wet or dry. Walking on the steep side of a chalk down is entirely different in wet and dry weather, and as you walk it you will undoubtedly envisage fighting on it. Look for the local hazard: the clump of thorn bushes, the sharp little slope, the spongy patch near a spring or stream, and the ground which looks smooth from a short distance but which is very rough and disconcerting when you are on it.

You needed an iron nerve to fight in these early battles. As you moved up towards the enemy you were encouraged by the competent look of your fellow soldiers, and the exhortations of your leaders. This was easy enough. When the enemy came in sight there probably seemed to be rather more of them than you had expected. The front lines would meet. There would be noise, confusion and swaying of the first few ranks. For most of the army it would be a matter of watch and wait. Some would be pressing forward, eager to take their turn; others might not like what they saw, which was decidedly less pleasant and easy than they had been led to expect. These – not many perhaps – might perhaps decide to drop to the rear and slip away, but in most battles that would have been foreseen. There would be a ring of medieval 'military police' waiting at the rear to take care of just that contingency, and the less resolute would reluctantly realize that the only way out of the battle was through the front. Later when the battle was being decided and most men were fighting for their lives some might take that chance to disappear. Their subsequent account of the battle would doubtless explain both the significant part they had taken in it and the miracle by which they had survived. But there would be no one to contradict the details. If you really got into the thick of it in a medieval battle, you would be exceptionally lucky if you came out to tell the tale.

One very good way of understanding what went on in a battle is to play it out as a war-game. War-gamers set out their toy soldiers and weapons on a model of the battlefield. They then throw a dice in turn to decide what moves each can make. The rules are quite complicated and some battles go on for days. (See *Charge* [a manual for war-gamers] by Brig. P. Young and Lt-Col. J. P. Lawford.) The most interesting part of the game is the light it throws on the battle. You may have heard that in a certain battle the numbers were 50,000 and the area over which it was fought was two square miles. By the time the battle is fought as a war-game, the size, shape, and surface of the battleground will probably be well known. Even if it is not the mere extent of the battlefield may throw some doubt on the original contemporary accounts. It will be clear that there is a limit to the number of troops who could have been engaged on any piece of ground. Perhaps you will make precisely the same calculations – and mistakes – as the original commanders. But you will not suffer for them as they did.

Were these ancient warriors so different from ourselves? Were they immune from fear, pain, discomfort? Not so very different and not immune from anything. The Saxon soldier, the Briton, the Norman, the Cavalier, the Roundhead: they were harder than untrained men today but not necessarily tougher than the elite of modern armies. Over and over again it is training and discipline which tells, and there are many men in today's regiments who would have given as good as they got in those long-past battles.

THE BATTLE OF
MOUNT BADON

AD 516

The Battle of Mount Badon or Mons Badonicus has been somewhat of a mystery for over fifteen hundred years. Records are scanty and there has been much speculation over its exact site. It was an enormously important battle, and its result delayed the subjugation of Britain for fifty years. It was undoubtedly a masterpiece of strategic and tactical planning. Perhaps much of the mystery stems from the fact that Badon was chronicled by scholars and monks who were far away in time as well as place, and did not know the area in which it was reputedly fought. Looking at it today with no special prejudices to air, and being concerned only with what the late Col. A. H. Burne so aptly called IMP (Inherent Military Probability), the obscurity of Badon seems a little less impenetrable. Col. Burne's contribution to the study of ancient battlefields was invaluable but this does not of course mean that one would always agree with his deductions. Here we agree on the site but differ on the disposition of the forces and the course of events. Col. Burne accepts most of Geoffrey of Monmouth's account (written in the twelfth century) though he acknowledges that on other matters Geoffrey's versions were somewhat imaginative.

The visitor to any battlefield will first ask who fought it and why. Once this is established the course of the battle – even the choice of site – becomes much more obvious. To understand Badon we have to return in history nearly a hundred years before it occurred.

Badon was fought in 516 and was a battle between Saxons and Britons. The Britons were the inhabitants of these islands when the Romans landed in 55 BC. After the Romans had been in occupation for nearly five hundred years the Britons had become soft and unaccustomed to warfare. Long before the Roman legions finally left Britain in the first half of the fifth century a new force had appeared on the scene. This was the Saxons. They had first appeared in the Channel as early as the second century AD. They were great fighters and sea-farers and, when they settled, skilful farmers. The Romans had a healthy respect for them and even admired them but had created a special command to deal with their marauding. It was under the 'Count of the Saxon Shore' and he had a fleet of warships and a chain of forts to help him in his task. The Romans are always thought of as a land-based people swinging along their magnificent roads to confront the enemy in set-piece battles. But the Romans were flexible and adaptable, and had mastered many sorts of fighting. They were not too proud to adopt the techniques and camouflage of their opponents if it seemed likely to bring success. And it usually did. They even painted themselves, partly for camouflage, partly to inspire fear.

But the Romans had too many troubles at home to be able to stay and protect Britain from the Saxons. The Roman empire was rotten within, and slowly but inexorably the out-posts were withdrawn. As the legions left Britain other would-be conquerors were waiting to take their place. The Caledonians – the Picts – were ready to swarm over the walls which the Romans had built to keep them out – the Antonine Wall, and Hadrian's Wall. The future looked ominous for the Britons who had been protected so long.

There were other threats than these. Swarming in from the north and west was another intensely warlike people – the Scots. At first they raided the Midlands and the south but later they moved north-east, settled, and gave their name to Scotland.

The Romans had done almost everything in Britain except teach them to defend themselves. They had made roads and cities, built houses, developed agriculture and mining, and even imprinted their own civilization on their subject people.

It is not perhaps entirely fair to blame the subsequent defeat of the Britons on their lack of military experience during the Roman occupation. Many Britons had served in the Roman legions, and were as skilled and brave as their fellows in arms. But courage and skill are no substitute for numbers if the opponents are no less able, unless that courage and skill can be used behind adequate fortifications, or adapted to an entirely different mode of warfare. This the Britons did not appreciate early enough or widely enough. But on one occasion they did use exactly the right tactics against their opponents and that was at Mount Badon.

The last Roman legions were withdrawn from Britain in 410 AD. Soon the Jutes arrived and settled in Kent. The situation was not entirely clear-cut. The Jutes had arrived by invitation but had quarrelled with their hosts and driven them out. They demanded the south-east. There were still Romans in Britain but they had no military power. In the *Anglo-Saxon Chronicle*, our source for the sequence of the main events, we read:

443 In this year the Britons sent across the sea to Rome and begged for help against the Picts, but they got none there, for the Romans were engaged in a campaign against Attila, King of the Huns. And then they sent to the Angles, and made the same request of the chieftains of the English.

Unfortunately for the Britons the hoped-for saviours proved to be the next aggressors. At first their visits were no real threat but in 477 the formidable Aelle arrived with his three sons. 'They killed many Britons and drove some into flight.' Aelle was clearly a warrior king whose principal pastime was making himself an intolerable nuisance to his neighbours far and near. He found Britain a tempting target with people to be conquered and rich land to be plundered and occupied. One of his sons, Wlencing, gave his name to Lancing, near Shoreham, and another, Cissa, to Chichester. The Britons made the fatal mistake of trying to hold him off from fixed defences with no sally-ports. They allowed themselves to be besieged in the old Roman fort of Anderida, now called Pevensey. As a base for the Romans under the command of the Count of the Saxon Shore, Anderida had had many advantages when the Roman fleet patrolled the Channel and the walls of Anderida could hold a large mobile striking force. But Anderida was not a place in which to be trapped as the unfortunate Britons soon found. Aelle and Cissa besieged it, captured it, and killed every man, woman and child within the walls.

Pevensey is a fortress which has seen plenty of action and much blood spilt. Those who visit it today will find the ruins of a Norman castle in a corner of the Roman walls, and that castle also saw some severe fighting during the Middle Ages. Nearly a thousand years later, Pevensey was cunningly adapted for anti-invasion warfare, for in 1940, when a German landing was expected, gun emplacements were built and blended deceptively into the old walls. They may be inspected today.

After the massacre at Pevensey, Aelle founded the Kingdom of the South Saxons, which became known as Sussex.

From then onwards, the Saxons arrived in increasing numbers. Some landed farther west, and founded the Kingdom of the West Saxons or Wessex; others founded Essex, the county of the East Saxons. Angles, Saxons and Jutes all came from contiguous areas and it is surprising that the early chroniclers managed to distinguish them. All were formidable in war, but none more than the Saxons whose achievements were only too well known on the Continent. One of our sources is Gildas, a sixth-century monk. Describing their effect on Britain he wrote:

famine dire and most famous sticks to the wandering and staggering people, priests and people swords on every side gleaming and flames crackling were together mown to the ground . . . fragments of bodies covered with clots as if congealing of purple-coloured blood, mixed in a sort of fearful winepress, and burial of any kind there was none except the ruins of houses, the bellies of beasts and birds, in the open . . .

At first the Britons could do little except flee or stand and be slaughtered. Many chose to take their chance in the woods, for there was no safety in the towns the Romans had left. The Saxons did not occupy the buildings they had not troubled to destroy; this concept of civilized life was beyond their grasp, but they used the Roman roads to penetrate deep and wide into Britain. Out of their misery the Britons had to evolve a new form of life and warfare. Like their ancestors of some five hundred years before they began to display the skills of guerilla fighting which had impressed the first Roman invaders. We know from Roman accounts that the Britons were highly mobile, could race around in chariots, alight, fight, and leap back on to their horses and chariots. But these skills had long been forgotten, and were never completely revived. Instead the Britons developed a more cautious form of warfare, with a technique for ambushing the isolated or unwary. They were slow to learn the lesson of avoiding pitched battles and we read (in the *Anglo-Saxon Chronicle*) such laconic statements as:

495   In this year two chieftains, Cerdic and his son Cynric came with five ships to Britain at the place which is called Cerdicesora, and they fought against the Britons on the same day.
501   In this year Port and his two sons Bieda and Maegla came to Britain with two ships at the place which is called Portsmouth and there they killed a young British man of very high rank.
508   In this year Cerdic and Cynric killed a British king whose name was Natanleod and 5000 men with him, and the land right up to Charford was called Netley after him.
514   In this year the West Saxons came with three ships at a place which is called Cerdicesora and Stuf and Wihtgah fought against the Britons and put them to flight.

These early battles were strenuous and bloody enough to impress the chroniclers but they were not decisive. The Saxon invaders would celebrate their victories with plunder and senseless destruction but at that stage had little in the way of constructive ideas for consolidating their gains. Had the

Britons been well led they could have ambushed these marauders on their return to the coast, and recaptured most of the spoils. But, apart from certain isolated occasions, they seldom did so. The Saxons either set sail for their homeland or settled near the coast in this new country.

Many of the Britons had fled far beyond the farthest point of Saxon penetration, deep though that was in places. The Saxons referred to all the Britons as the 'Waelisch', which meant foreigners, and this, in time, gave the name to the country where some Britons settled and survived – Wales. But before Wales became a country much more blood was spilt and it was by no means all British.

By this time the Britons had been driven to desperation. Gildas's account of their misfortunes is substantiated by Bede who wrote:

Consequently some of the miserable remnants, being taken in the mountains, were slain in heaps. Others, constrained by hunger coming forward, yielded hands to their foes to undergo for the sake of food perpetual slavery, if indeed they were not immediately killed. Others, sorrowing, sought countries over sea. Others, remaining in the fatherland, led a wretched life in mountains, woods, and steep crags, always with apprehensive mind.

But, it is a constant fact of military situations that matters are seldom as bad as they seem, or for that matter as good as they might be. It is obvious to us nowadays with our long experience of guerilla warfare that, if a conquered people are determined, they can first of all make life very hazardous and unpleasant for their conquerors, and then, when enough time has passed, defeat them. But to do both they need leaders.

Guerilla warfare, to use the modern term, can be waged from two very different bases. It can be mounted from a town where the resistance fighter is able to hide himself in a crowd, or it can be waged by ambush from retreats in the woods. The second form has usually been the most popular, though not necessarily the most productive of results. Living in the woods, surrounded by trusted companions, can rapidly develop into a complacent and inactive comradeship. Robin Hoods have existed in many countries, and in many centuries, and few of them have been more than a minor nuisance to the government in power. In sixth-century Britain it was easy to be an inactive Robin Hood. Apart from the trackways and uplands most of the country was wood and thicket; today it is not easily realized how dense uncleared thicket can become in a few years, or how dangerous marshy low-lying areas rapidly become when drainage is neglected. Little of the land had been cleared in Roman times, and by 516 over a hundred years had passed since those peaceful days. Even after centuries of intensive clearance and agriculture, a hundred years of neglect would make much of England un-recognizable, if not impassable. Anyone who has any doubts about this should go and look at a garden – there are plenty around – which has not been touched for a year pending speculative building, or 'development' as it is now flatteringly called. The Britons would have had no shortage of inaccessible hideouts; but their problem would have been to find the leaders to organize resistance, train their scattered bands, and mount an effective counter-attack. The weakness of guerilla forces is that if they can be tempted to stand and fight on open ground they tend to disintegrate.

But the Britons had a leader – a man of genius. Some called him Arthur, others Ambrosius Aurelianus. There has been much learned debate as to who Arthur may have been, but for the purposes of this battle it does not greatly matter. Whether the Briton general was named Ambrosius Aurelianus, or Arthur, can never now be established. One theory is that 'Arthur' was the name by which Ambrosius Aurelianus was known. It is unlikely that the rank and file Briton referred to his leader as King Ambrosius Aurelianus. Ambrosius was a Roman aristocrat whose parents had settled in Britain and had been murdered by the Saxons. He had missed being killed himself and had built up a resistance force. Guerilla leaders seldom use their true names. Gildas describes him thus:

Ambrosius Aurelianus being leader, a modest man, who alone by chance of the Roman nation had survived in the collision of so great a storm, his parents doubtless clad in the purple, having been killed in the same, whose progeny now in our times having greatly degenerated from their ancestral excellence, to whom, the Lord assenting, victory fell.

Bede put it rather more coherently:

But when the hostile army [the Saxons], having destroyed and dispersed the natives of the island had returned home, the Britons by degrees to resume strength and spirit, emerging from the hiding places, wherein they had concealed themselves, and with one accord imploring celestial help lest they should be destroyed even to extermination. They had at that time for their leader Ambrosius Aurelianus, a modest man, who alone by chance of the Roman nation had survived the aforesaid storm, his parents, bearing a royal and distinguished name, having been killed in the same. Under this leader therefore the Britons took heart, and challenging their victors to battle obtain the victory by the help of God.

'A modest man'. Great generals often are, though not, of course, invariably. There is, of course, no reason to believe that Arthur and Ambrosius were not different people, that the former had his headquarters at Glastonbury, and trained his forces in Cornwall, to which the Saxons had not penetrated, and that Ambrosius was based in North Wales, where he became an expert at hill-fighting. But it is just possible that they were the same man, and the scraps of folklore which have passed down, of the Round Table, of trusted counsellors, and a symbolic sword which only the born, bred, and educated leader could wield, all seem in keeping.

The Latin meaning of Ambrosius is 'immortal', and the name lingers on in the Welsh 'Emrys'. Aurelianus means 'golden'. Arthur is thought to derive from the Celtic word for 'the bear' – a not unsuitable name for a guerilla leader.

We see from the *Anglo-Saxon Chronicle* that the main Saxon raids were separated by several years. There would be a raid, a battle or two, and the return to the homeland or the shoreline, as described above. The first Saxons had neither the administration nor logistical support to mount a long campaign into areas where the opposition was unknown and food supplies would be precarious to say the least. But in 516 – which is an approximate date, for Gildas says it was the year of his birth – a Saxon force of considerable strength was moving west along the Ermine Way (between Silchester and Swindon). It was reputed to have been led by one Aelle but this can hardly have been the Aelle who had first appeared in 477. But whether Aelle or one of his descendants, and whether 516 or twenty years earlier it makes no difference; it was a tough, resourceful fighting force which was probing north-west along the Ermine Way. Perhaps they were a little nervous at being so far from their base : they should have been. But as mile succeeded mile along this Roman road, beautifully straight, and not a Briton in sight, it looked as if the Saxon reputation had cleared the way before them. They had no reason to use scouts or proceed cautiously. At the end of this stage of the road there was said to be another old Roman town, and beyond that the sea again. They were right. Swindon lay ahead and also what would become known as the Bristol Channel. But so, unknown to them, did Ambrosius and his Britons.

As they approached Badon it looked no different from anywhere else along the route. They were, as it happened, at a point which had seen other and bitter battles. They marched along the plateau, down the dip, and up the slope into what is now Baydon village. When they were half-way up that slope, the trap was sprung. It is not difficult to reconstruct the probable sequence of events. Possibly two swift flank attacks from the cover which is still close to the road today, perhaps another force directly in front, possibly cavalry which would send the Saxons reeling back down the hill, and probably an attack around the rear over the route they had just covered;

this would make sure that once tumbled to the bottom of the dip they would stay there. It would be a difficult position for the Saxons to fight their way out of.

Nennius, a ninth-century historian, whose accuracy is considered more doubtful than most of the early historians, stated that Arthur was the victor of Badon and that it was the last of twelve consecutive victories. He gives the Saxon casualties as 440. There is no reason to believe that this figure is anything but a wild guess, as indeed many battle casualty figures even of recent battles often are. But at least he does not number them in thousands as many early historians tend to do.

Possibly the total Saxon force was 3000. This 'army' would be spread out along the road. The Britons would doubtless have liked to have caught them all in the trap but this, even with the advantage of greater numbers, would have been impossible. But once the initial ambush had succeeded, with devastating effect, the Britons would fade away into the undergrowth. The Saxon rear party would then come up, perhaps bury the dead but certainly halt and take stock in Badon itself. It would have been a severe and costly shock but doubtless they decided that the Britons had done their best but lost heart and given up. There was no reason why they should not press on, though perhaps cautiously.

The next day they did so. About five miles on from Baydon the Ermine Way is crossed by the Ridgeway, which will figure again in this book in subsequent battles. The Ridgeway was one of the great strategic roadways of Britain. It stretches through Wiltshire and Berkshire and then links up with the even older Icknield Way which goes right through to the Wash. Some parts of this ancient trackway are now modern roads, with tarmac, signs, and heavy traffic; other parts are almost as wild as they were a thousand and more years ago – it was an old road even in Roman times – and the rambler who tramps along the lonelier parts of it will feel that perhaps he is not so far removed from the feelings of earlier travellers.

But most of the users of the Ridgeway had considerably less romantic thoughts about it than the modern rambler. To the

Roman legionary, to the Briton, and to many another it was as glamorous as Queen's Avenue, Aldershot, is to a modern soldier. To the Saxons who suddenly came across this important trackway crossing their own it betokened much, and none of it romantic. This showed why they had been ambushed at Baydon; this was the highway on which the Britons linked up. And where there is a crossroads the chances are that there is a means of defending it.

They proceed to look for this strongpoint. Less than a mile to the east they find it. It is Liddington Castle, an Iron-Age fort on a 900-foot hill. It has a useful high bank and ditch, and on the hill slopes are traces of other works which made the path of the attacker hazardous. Here, it seems, the Saxons located the rest of the force which had inflicted such damage on them the previous day. Perhaps there had been another brush at the crossroads and the Saxons had been led in pursuit to Liddington. Up till recent times Liddington was known as Badbury castle, i.e. the burgh at Bade.

The second phase of the battle and indeed the first is some-what confused by the fact that some writers — notably Geoffrey of Monmouth — considered that the Saxons occupied the hill fort and the Britons were attacking them. This seems less than probable — to put it mildly. It seems more likely that the Saxons, thinking they had come to the last stronghold of the Britons in that area, were determined to wipe them out and avenge the previous day's defeat. As they pressed to the assault they would find this 900-foot hill a tougher proposition than they had expected. But once committed there would be no thought of drawing back. And once more the cavalry for which both Ambrosius and Arthur were famous would come into action. Some think that much of the battle took place on the open ground between Liddington and Badbury. Perhaps the last stages did, when the Saxons had been flung back from the hill slopes, retired to the hollow field below it on the north side, and then, tired and dispirited, were cut to pieces by the British cavalry coming from either side of the Ridgeway.

Geoffrey of Monmouth (several hundred years later)

describes the Saxon slain as being 'many thousands'. Whatever the number it was undoubtedly most of their force.
Doubtless a few survived to tell the story of disaster – a few
always do, and the tale loses nothing in the telling. But it
would soon be obvious enough to the Saxons what had
happened: their invasion army, which was the strongest which
could be mustered, had been annihilated. It was clear that if
that had been the fate of what had looked like an all-
conquering army, central Britain was best left alone for the
time being. It was forty years before the *Anglo-Saxon
Chronicle* records Saxons in Wiltshire again. In 552 Cynric
'fought against the Britons at a place called Salisbury'. It is
not recorded as a Saxon victory but only as a fight. In all
probability it was an attempt by the Saxons to capture the
ancient earthwork fortress of Old Sarum, and anyone who
looks at the banks and ditches of Old Sarum today will not
envy them their task. Presumably they by-passed it because,
in 556, they are recorded as fighting against the Britons at
Barbury. This was Cynric and Ceawlin at the battle of Beranburgh just north of Barbury Castle (another Iron-Age fort).
Beranburgh is marked on the 172 (Swindon and Devizes) map
at 147 769. It looks a slightly improbable site for a battlefield
as the Saxons would have had to pass by the hill without
attacking and being attacked, and then been caught on the
flat plain in front. However, it is an important nodal point
where six roads meet, and even if one doubts the actual site
there can be no question that plenty of battles, large and small,
must have been fought in the area.

But no other battle compares with the achievement of
Badon. There the flower and pride of the Saxon army was
outwitted, crushed, and finally destroyed by a conglomerate
force which behaved with superb discipline, and was clearly
expertly led. No wonder accounts of it survived in Welsh
epic poetry. At every stage it was adroitly handled – as the
Saxons would ruefully have agreed had they survived to tell
the tale.

THE BATTLE OF
DYRHAM
(originally Deorham)

AD 577

In spite of the setbacks of Badon, in the year 516, the Saxons were making steady progress and consolidating their gains elsewhere in Britain. Now they were coming as settlers; now too they were beginning to have a better appreciation of the potential of the country they were conquering. By this time they had been in contact with Britain for three hundred years. Much can happen in that space of time; it is perhaps hardly credible that it is only just over three hundred years since Cavaliers and Roundheads were fighting a bitter civil war in this country. The progress of the Saxons can hardly be compared with that in Britain between the seventeenth and twentieth centuries but it would be equally wrong to imagine them as the same in the third century AD as in the sixth.

Some time in the sixth century – it is impossible to estimate when – Saxons occupied the deserted city of London, which became the country of the Middle Saxons, or Middlesex. So now we had Jutes in Kent, and Saxons in Essex, Sussex, Middlesex and Wessex, and probably also in Surrey (which means 'southern people'). The Angles had given their name to East Anglia, where there were the North Folk and South Folk. Above the Humber they had created the Kingdom of Northumbria, the northern part being known as Bernicia and the southern part, which is now mainly Yorkshire, being given the name of Deira. Combined forces from these areas had forced their way into the Midlands to create Mercia. Mercia was a 'march', that is a border state, and it extended to what is now Staffordshire. Beyond that the Britons were in force and among their bases were Wroxeter and Chester. They were now calling themselves the *Cymru*, which means comrades.

In short the Anglo-Saxons now held the eastern half of the

country and some of the Midlands, and the Britons held the western parts, including Cornwall, Devon and Somerset, Wales, Gloucestershire, Herefordshire, Shropshire, and the north-west. This stalemate could continue almost indefinitely unless the invaders could effect a strategic breakthrough. It was necessary to cut a line through the British areas to the sea, and then widen it. Clearly it would be extremely difficult to do this in the north-west, though it would have to be done eventually. The obvious point for a drive forward was where Aelle had failed some forty years before.

By now some new names had appeared on the military scene. Ceawlin has already been mentioned in the previous chapter as having been in action at Barbury, in combination with Cynric who had put the Britons to flight at Salisbury four years previously (552). In 560 we read that Ceawlin succeeded to the Kingdom in Wessex and Aelle to the Kingdom of the Northumbrians. Some of these warrior kings traced their descent back to Woden (the god whose name is commemorated in Wednesday); doubtless they seemed worthy of their lineage.

Ceawlin was clearly an outstanding warrior. He and his brother Cutha sometimes fought side by side, at other times went on separate campaigns. In 568, says the *Anglo-Saxon Chronicle*, 'Ceawlin and Cutha fought against Ethelbert and drove him in flight into Kent.' Ethelbert was a powerful king and this was no mean achievement. Doubtless the quarrel had sprung from a border incident. Three years later we hear of Cutha again.

571   In this year Cutha fought against the Britons at Biedcanford and captured four towns: Limbury, Aylesbury, Bensington and Eynsham, and in the same year he died.

This campaign of Cutha's is an interesting one. It looks as if he had gathered up a force in East Anglia and then driven south-west through Bedford and Aylesbury, reached the Thames at Benson just north of Wallingford, and then travelled along the river to Eynsham. Here he would be on

the edge of Briton-held country, and the opposition would
be too strong for him to continue. Perhaps he had been
wounded, or the effects of the Thames Valley marshes proved
more deadly than British swords, for he died at the end of
this successful campaign.

But as one warrior fell and was laid ceremonially to rest
there were a dozen others ready to take his place. Often they
bore the same name or names remarkably like their predecessors. Four years after Cutha's great campaign, which
nearly cut right across England from east to west, another
great probe is on the way to an even more significant victory.
The *Anglo-Saxon Chronicle* has the laconic entry:

577 In this year Cuthwine and Ceawlin fought against
the Britons and killed three kings, Conmail, Condidan and
Farinmail, at the place which is called Dyrham; and they
captured three of their cities, Gloucester, Cirencester and
Bath.

The statement is in the best tradition of cryptic war
despatches, such as 'I came, I saw, I conquered.'

Doubtless the Anglo-Saxons had now got the measure of
the situation. Possibly they had sailed around the coasts and
formed a very fair idea of the strength and weakness of the
British position. If Cutha's thrust could have been sustained
it would have struck at almost precisely the same point as
Ceawlin reached. But now it was Ceawlin's turn. We do not
know anything about his preliminary moves but we do know
that during the previous twenty years this king of Wessex
had gradually been pushing towards the north-west of his
kingdom. There must have been hundreds of skirmishes and
ambushes and raids in those years and all the while Ceawlin
was consolidating his position, building an army and getting
ready for the drive forward. But, on the other side, the fighting men were no novices. They knew well enough what was in
train, and what was in Ceawlin's mind. Under normal conditions the kings of Bath, Cirencester, and Gloucester would
have been happily fighting each other, disputing some border

territory or other. But misery makes strange bedfellows, and Conmail, Condidan and Farinmail had held their strategic and tactical conferences. By a stroke of good fortune Ceawlin's invasion route led right through the centre of their territories so there could be no question of one fighting for his life while another stood idly by pondering when or where to intervene – if at all. A look at the map shows that Ceawlin was planning to slip through the middle of their strongholds to break through on to the Severn estuary at Berkeley. But the movements of his large army would doubtless have been faithfully reported by scouts and spies, and even though he had slipped past Bath there must have been a huge force waiting to confront him somewhere. As it happened, it was at Dyrham, but it was in a badly-chosen position.

Nobody knows exactly how Ceawlin advanced to Dyrham but it is a fair assumption that he came from Melksham to Box and on to Marshfield. He could perhaps have gone via Chippenham but that would have made his approach too obvious. Approaching by Marshfield he still had the option of cutting back south and west and reaching the Severn near Weston. He would have had to fight sooner or later, and doubtless he wished for nothing better, but a good general calculates his chances and takes a risk well aware that his opponent is also calculating – and miscalculating – too. But even Ceawlin must have drawn in his breath when he came to Dyrham and wondered who would be standing victor on that battlefield by nightfall.

A look at the map suggests that Ceawlin had brought his army through West Littleton. He may have thought that his three principal opponents were mainly intent upon guarding their own cities but, as it proved, they had concentrated their forces at the point he was almost certain to try to pass – Hinton Hill. Needless to say there have been a host of other theories about approach routes he might have chosen but they all lead to Hinton Hill.

It was a good defensive position but like all defensive positions it had its drawbacks. It overlooked a key crossing on the approach road to both Bath and Bristol but was of value only as an untakeable base, and even then for a limited period only. When an army takes up a defensive position several consequences are immediately set in train. The first is that although the strongpoint gives a temporary feeling of immunity it also diminishes the sort of aggressive morale which is necessary for a field victory. The second effect is that one might be tempted out of a rugged position and then caught by a swift attack which sends one's army floundering among the very obstacles on which one was relying to upset the enemy. If the enemy decides to try to slip by, it is necessary to attack at some point before his army has crossed the line you are planning to hold. Furthermore, if the enemy decides to besiege you at this point he has the resources of the countryside to draw on while you have your stores only, and in sixth-century Britain these would not be very extensive. The last and greatest liability is that you may be surrounded and with morale at zero point have to fight to the end hoping to kill enough to destroy the attack or, alternatively, to break out.

It looks as if Ceawlin's warriors were first confronted about 300 yards ahead of the camp position. The technique of this type of fighting varies little from country to country and age to age. The attacking troops send their front line to crash forward as far as they can go, then stand aside – if still alive – to let the second rank stream through the gaps they have made. Defensive troops on the other hand try to check the onslaught a few hundred yards ahead of their lines, either by ditches or fortifications full of resolute men, and then, if and when the line wavers, put in a heavier attack if it seems appropriate. From that moment the course of the battle becomes highly unpredictable, depending on the skill of one commander and the rashness of another. A commander with a strong hold on his troops can afford to let them press on knowing he can withdraw them if needed; one with lesser discipline would be ill-advised to do so for he might not see them again, if ever, till the battle was over.

The joint command does not seem to have worked very successfully once the first blows were struck. There is always a chance when keen rivals band together for mutual defence that one group will cheerfully let another take more than its share of the enemy without doing much to take off the pressure. The Britons would have had bows but these were not as formidable as they would become later. Their armour was light, and on the Roman model, but it is unlikely that many would have possessed it. The Saxon rank and file had no armour at all, but their leaders usually had a chain-mail shirt and an iron framework helmet. They had spears, bows and shields. The spears – on both sides – were simple seven-foot shafts with iron heads, which could be used for thrusting or thrown like a javelin. Spears were handled with great dexterity for they were the principal weapon for hunting; an arrow was less reliable. Sometimes a man would loose off an arrow and if he missed be hard put to get in a spear-thrust. A spear was a more reliable weapon than a bow.

The sword was much beloved, and some swords were very richly ornamented. They were about thirty-three inches long, without much taper or point but with a keen edge on each side. The hand was partly protected by a cross-bar and the end of the hilt was a pommel, a rounded knob that helped to keep the hand from slipping off; it also gave balance to the blade. The balance of a weapon is a curious quality, but when it is right for the user he will twirl spear, javelin or axe like a tennis-racquet. After the first exchange of spears and arrows at Dyrham it was undoubtedly close-quarter fighting. The Saxons, whose numbers were probably greater than had been anticipated, would soon be fanning out around the hill, perhaps climbing more swiftly than expected. Here the Britons were too much on the defensive, and they lacked a single general of genius. Ceawlin was the veteran of a hundred encounters. He loved fighting – as all his nation did – but he fought to win. Somewhere, once, there was a detailed account of this battle, but today we only have the place, the result, and the names of three 'Kings' of whose existence we would not otherwise have known, for their names are in no other records. But even without that account, from what we know of what happened before and after and from an examination of the ground, it is not difficult to bring the vital battle of Deorham once again to life.

Ceawlin was through to the Severn. He captured Gloucester, Cirencester and Bath with ease, for most of the usual defenders of these former Roman towns were lying dead on the slopes of Hinton Hill. But his fighting life was only half over. He had split the Waelisch (the Britons) and from now onwards some would be in Cornwall and the West, and even in Brittany, while the others would be in Wales and the north-west. But there were plenty of people left to fight. Seven years after Dyrham the *Anglo-Saxon Chronicle* reports him as being in north Oxfordshire.

584   In this year Ceawlin and Cutha fought against the Britons at the place which is called Fethanleag and Cutha was killed there, and Ceawlin captured many villages and countless spoils and in anger returned to his own land.

Fethanleag was probably Fringford, a village four and a half miles north of Bicester. Historians have avoided comment on the reason for the Saxons fighting a battle in this place or the possible course of it but as it is on the old Roman road it is fairly obvious that this is where they marched head-on into the East Anglians. Ceawlin continued to fight but his great triumphs were over. In 592, 'Gregory succeeded to the Papacy at Rome. And in this year there occurred a great slaughter at "Woden's barrow" and Ceawlin was driven out.' Woden's Barrow is now called Adam's Grave. It is at Alton Priors, Wiltshire. Finally comes the last significant entry.

593   In this year Ceawlin, Cwichelm and Crida perished. And Aethelfrith succeeded to the kingdom.

Ceawlin undoubtedly died with his sword in his hand but where, by whom he was slain, and how he died will never be known. There are plenty of possibilities. Four years later we hear that his successor 'continually fought and contended against the English or the Britons or the Picts or the Scots'. It must have been sad for Ceawlin to die at that moment with all those splendid enemies to fight.

THE BATTLE OF ELLANDUN

AD 825

Like all early battles Ellandun is still somewhat of a mystery. The exact site was not recorded, nor the numbers involved, nor the casualties; we do, of course, know the result. Nevertheless, by the use of information about previous and later events it is possible to make very close deductions about Ellandun. But even if we had a full and detailed account of Ellandun – and other battles – it would not fully explain them in isolation any more than the Battle of Alamein in 1942 would be comprehensible if separated from the background of the Second World War. The only way to understand Ellandun is to take a brief look at the events of the 248 years since the vital strategic battle of Dyrham had been fought in 577.

Although the first stages of the Anglo-Saxon conquest of Britain had already taken over one hundred and fifty years of steady fighting the Britons were still strongly entrenched in Wales, in the area west of the Pennines, and also in Cornwall. Ceawlin's breakthrough to the Severn estuary in 577 had been a major strategic gain but even with this setback the Britons were still a formidable force. This did not worry the Saxons, who had their hands full with using the lands they already occupied. The Saxons regarded fighting as a natural and desirable part of life, so the presence of hostile Britons on their borders seemed by no means unusual or unwelcome. The pace of conquest was partly dictated by logistical problems and partly by the need to keep a watchful eye on the activities of one's comrades in arms and fellow-countrymen; there was not much point in occupying fresh territory if a neighbour took advantage of your absence to raid your homelands.

The next stride forward for the Saxon conquest came in AD 604 (or perhaps 605 or 606). This was the great battle of

Chester. (The Romans had called the town Deva, but after they had left many Roman cities came to be known as 'ceasters' and later as 'chesters' or 'casters'. Thus we find Winchester, Worcester, Colchester, Doncaster, etc., although these were not the names by which the Romans knew them.)

The battle of Chester became possible because Aethelfrith of Bernicia (northern Northumbria) had crushed his neighbour the King of Deira (southern Northumbria – approximately the area of modern Yorkshire). Aethelfrith was a formidable, utterly ruthless warrior. Two years before his Chester campaign he had had a devastating victory over the Scots at what is thought to have been Dawston in Liddesdale. His own Saxon army sustained heavy losses but the Scots were annihilated; the *Anglo-Saxon Chronicle* bluntly states that no king of the Scots ever afterwards dared to lead an army against Northumbria. Events subsequently proved it wrong but the chronicler was a historian not a prophet. The exact site of the battle is not known but this does not mean that it is undiscoverable. All over England there are many areas which are known to have been battlefields; one day perhaps a combination of military historians, archaeologists and local folklorists may produce interesting theories about some of these sites.

The King of all Northumbria and conqueror of the Scots then took his army to the west:

Aethelfrith led his army to Chester and there killed a countless number of Britons and thus was fulfilled Augustine's prophecy by which he said 'If the Britons do not wish to have peace with us, they shall perish at the hands of the Saxons.' There were also killed 200 priests who had come there to pray for the army of the Britons. Their leader was called Brocmail and he escaped with fifty men.

Although we can only estimate the numbers involved this must have been a tremendous battle. The Britons, well aware of the threat to their position, had put a combined force from Wales and Cumbria into the field. Undoubtedly there was a split in the command and the direction of the battle but even with this the Britons must have put up a desperate fight. The presence of the priests on the battlefield shows the determination with which the Britons approached the contest; it was not the first nor the last time that clerics would appear on battlefields and be massacred for their trouble, but it is not a pleasant thought. Aethelfrith had no doubt assumed that their presence in the fighting area had invalidated their status as non-combatants, if indeed he thought so deeply of it at all. More probably he saw them as the evil exponents of a spurious religion which should be eradicated. The Saxons had recently been converted to Christianity, and doubtless regarded themselves as the defenders of their new faith. The *Chronicle* states:

601   In this year Gregory sent the pallium [archbishop's cloak, denoting episcopal authority] to Britain to Archbishop Augustine, and many religious teachers to his assistance; and Bishop Paulinus who converted Edwin, King of the Northumbrians, to baptism.

Perhaps Aethelfrith, who was Edwin's son, thought he was fighting a Holy War. Like many converts to a religion he would be more zealous for his religion than those who had been born in it. Furthermore Aethelfrith's view of his Christian duty was unlikely to have included a merciful attitude to the spiritual comforters of his opponents, particularly as the Augustinians would have stressed their iniquities.

The Saxons were by no means a homogeneous people. In 607 the King of Wessex is reported as fighting against the South Saxons and, as it was significant enough to be recorded in the *Anglo-Saxon Chronicle*, this was clearly no border skirmish. The next King of Wessex remained on the throne for thirty-one years. In 614 he was involved in a major battle at Beandun, and killed 2045 Britons. Times were turbulent and unsettled; heathenism returned in Kent and Middlesex. The power struggle went on. Aethelfrith, the victor of Dawston and Chester, at last met his match – or perhaps merely bad luck – in 617. He was killed by Raedwald, King of the East Angles. His successor, Edwin, banished all of Aethelfrith's sons before going on to conquer the rest of Saxon England, except Kent.

Christianity did not appear to have a markedly restraining influence on the Saxon rulers in their petty kingdoms. The conquest of the remainder of Britain became secondary to establishing who was paramount chief among the settled portions. Apart from the need to keep a watchful eye on any upstarts in one's own domains the Saxon king had to be ever vigilant against being swallowed by his neighbour, and preferably to avoid it by himself making an aggressive move. These moves took many forms and at times displayed a subtlety which is not uncharacteristic of the twentieth century. In the year 626 the King of Wessex sent an assassin to kill King Edwin of Northumbria. The plot miscarried, for he killed two of the bodyguards but only wounded the King. The Saxons were by no means averse to a little treachery if it suited their purpose, but Edwin's reaction to the attempt to kill him was to boil with moral indignation. By a happy coincidence his wife had borne him a daughter on the night of the attempted assassination, and Edwin promised Paulinus, the new Bishop of Northumbria, that if Paulinus would pray to God for a victory over the King of Wessex he (Edwin) would give this same daughter to God's service. Paulinus prayed fervently and Edwin took a large army into Wessex. The result was all that could be desired. Edwin won a devastating victory in Wessex and killed five minor kings; in return for this divine favour he built first a wooden and then a stone church at York. He had not however killed the right man, one Cwichelm, for we find the Wessex king fighting a drawn battle with the King of Mercia two years later. Otherwise Edwin thrived on his new religion; he acquired East Anglia and Essex from the dominion of Kent, he drove the Picts back beyond the Forth, and he even built a fleet on the west coast which enabled him to conquer the Isle of Man and Anglesey.

The title at which all these war lords were aiming was that

of Bretwalda. By this time the Saxon conquests had developed
into seven separate kingdoms, known collectively as the
Heptarchy. They were Wessex, Mercia, Northumbria, East
Anglia, Essex, Sussex, and Kent. Wessex, including what is
roughly known as south and south-western England, was the
most powerful, and the others gradually fell into that order
of importance though the lesser ones occasionally had their
moments of glory. The title of Bretwalda passed from
Northumbria to Kent, thence to Mercia, and thence to Wessex.
The details of this struggle for power do not concern us here
but it is necessary to know the trend of events if we are to
understand the battle which it brought about.

Edwin's growing power alarmed his rivals, but their reaction
was not to accept it as inevitable; instead they adopted determined counter-measures. The next two probable victims on
Edwin's march of conquest were Penda of Mercia and Cadwallon of Gwynedd (N. Wales). The former, who was a
relentless heathen, and the latter, who was allegedly a
Christian, found no problem over allying for their common
safety. Their combined force met and defeated Edwin's in
the Battle of Hatfield in 633. If this was Hatfield (Herts) it
was a curious place for him to be brought to battle by a
Midlander and a Welshman but perhaps they had noted his
exposed flank as he ventured so far from his base, perhaps
to conquer Middlesex and Kent, and they caught him at a
vital tactical point. But 'Hatfield' – which means an open
heath – might have been anywhere, and more probably was
somewhere between the Midlands and Yorkshire. After their
victory Cadwallon and Penda lost no time in invading
Northumbria where the former – and probably the latter –
were responsible for a series of cruelties which caused
comment even in those hardened times. Edwin's name is
commemorated by the town he founded 'Edwin's burgh', now
Edinburgh.

But, of course, fortune ebbed and flowed. Cadwallon's
ebbed right out when he was killed by Oswald who had raised
a combined force of Northumbrians and Scots and marched
south bearing the Cross as a standard. Readers of *British*

Battlefields: the North will recall that in 1138 the Cross, travelling in the opposite direction, won the Battle of the Standard for the English. Without his formidable Welsh ally, Penda was not strong enough to hold the northern areas but this did not mean that he was by any means a spent force. Penda seems to have been a remarkable person. According to the *Anglo-Saxon Chronicle* he did not succeed to his throne till he was fifty but he seems to have held it till he was eighty, when he was killed in battle. These figures have been disputed as being improbable but as everything about Penda was improbable – his intelligence, ingenuity, endurance and persistence – it does not seem entirely fair to dispute his age in that context. Penda seemed to believe that it is better to wear out than to rust out for when not fighting the Northumbrians he was busy killing off the kings of East Anglia on one side of his kingdom and wresting the lands of the Hwicce from Wessex on the other. The Hwicce were once a very powerful tribe whose territories formerly occupied the area of Worcestershire and Gloucestershire; now all they are remembered by is the Wychwood forest which preserves their name. Penda, although unable to reconquer Northumbria, still maintained a series of border wars with Oswald. In one of these, in 643, Oswald was killed at Oswestry (Oswald's tree). Possibly the tree was subsequently believed to have magical powers. Oswald had a reputation for holiness which extended well beyond Northumbria. His hands were buried at Bamburgh, where they did not decay, and many miracles were attributed to his relics. He was succeeded by his brother, Oswin, who ruled for twenty-eight years. He too was said to be a devout Christian but as he had his neighbour, Oswin of Deira, murdered after a disagreement it seems that he took his Christian obligations fairly lightly. Meanwhile Penda rampaged on elsewhere. In 645 he was reported as having put Cenwedh, King of Wessex, to flight, but did not succeed in killing him. The *casus belli* was that Cenwedh had deserted his sister; presumably the sister was Penda's not Cenwedh's and the latter had jilted her. The indefatigable Penda eventually met his match at Winwaedfeld, an unidentified battlefield thought to have been in Yorkshire. Oswin was his conqueror. Penda himself was killed, and with him thirty princes. If the dates are correct, Penda would then have been eighty – as mentioned earlier. It is by no means impossible. No ageing warrior would ever wish to die in bed and we have similar examples of ancient men on battlefields in Thurston of York at the Battle of the Standard, and the Earl of Northumberland at Bramham Moor though both were a few years younger than Penda was reputed to have been. Penda's 'elimination' removed the final obstacle to the religious conversion of Mercia. Thenceforth England was a Christian country. It also seemed as if Northumbria would now be the dominant kingdom, and the title of Bretwalda become theirs by hereditary right. Before Oswin died in 670 he had driven the Picts back to the Tay, extracted tribute from the Cumbrians and Welsh, and established a strong though decentralized grip on his Saxon sub-units. He was an early exploiter of the 'scorched earth' policy in that he kept the lands between Northumbria and Scotland so barren that not even a Pictish army could find sustenance on them.

His son was equally able. He captured Cumberland and Westmorland from the Britons and even invaded Ireland. Unluckily for him, for Northumbria, and for England generally, he was killed fighting the Picts in 685. His successors were of a different stamp. Their weaknesses were quickly recognized within and without Northumbria. The Picts were soon back and harrying the north – scorched earth or not – and the Mercians not only broke away but proceeded to establish a dominant kingdom themselves. They made East Anglia, Kent, and Essex dependent states, took the territory north of the Thames from Wessex, and even annexed Northumbrian lands south of the Trent.

As the years go by we receive fuller though still fragmentary entries in the *Anglo-Saxon Chronicle*. Readers will appreciate that though the *Chronicle* was begun in the ninth century, under orders from Alfred, there were several differing versions. In later years, after Alfred's death, this history of England became much more continuous. However, even in the early stages it gives us much useful information on which we may build up a picture of the composition, morale and motivation of Saxon armies. There is an illuminating account of local rivalries just before the great Offa of Mercia came to power. They concern Cynewulf, King of Wessex. Cynewulf and his counsellors of the West Saxons deprived his kinsman, Sigebehrt, of his kingdom (except for Hampshire) because of his unjust acts; he retained Hampshire until he killed the ealdorman who had stood by him the longest. At that point Cynewulf drove him out completely and he lived in the Weald until a swineherd stabbed him to death. The swineherd, it is recorded, was avenging the death of the ealdorman. This tribal, perhaps even domestic, loyalty explains how the Saxons kept their armies together. Presumably there was no lack of leadership nor discipline either.

Thirty-one years later Cynewulf was having trouble with one Cyneheard, who was the late Sigebehrt's younger brother. Cyneheard was the first to move. Learning that Cynewulf was at Merton visiting a mistress, he surrounded the house. Cynewulf heard the approach of unwelcome strangers and rushed to the door. Realizing that this was a plot to murder him, and that his thegns, his personal bodyguard, whom he had sent to a discreet distance, would not be able to help, he resolved to kill Cyneheard before he himself went under. He managed to wound the assassin but was himself struck down by many blows. The women screamed and the bodyguard heard. They rushed up but they too were outnumbered. Nevertheless, they died to a man, fighting like demons. The next day the rest of Cynewulf's thegns heard the news and came to the spot. There they found Cyneheard barricaded in, but very ready with rewards and promises if they would transfer their allegiance and support him as the new king. The thegns laughed the offer to scorn and set to. At the end of a desperate fight Cyneheard and his supporters were all dead except for one — and he was badly wounded.

Such loyalties and long memories are found in other primitive societies, but not all. Where they exist they account for much inter-tribal tension, even inter-family tension, but they ensure that when battles are fought they continue till one side has gained victory – probably at great cost – by annihilating the other. This then was the new phase of the Saxon wars, not as campaigns of adventure and conquest, but hard, relentless struggles against a competing unit, which might be another kingdom or merely a rival power faction.

In spite of the hazards of life in these early centuries, kings managed to have long reigns. Cynewulf, as we saw above, reigned for thirty-one years, and was somewhat unlucky to have his life ended then. Offa, the great king of Mercia, held his kingdom for thirty-nine years.

Offa might with justice be called the first King of England. He was more than the successful leader of a regional faction. All that we know of him shows the statesman, the strategist, and the man who was rightly respected in other countries. He corresponded with the great Charlemagne. He defeated and drove back the Welsh, as the Britons were now called, and he built a dyke from Chepstow in the south to a point two miles south of Prestatyn in the north. (Why he did not take it all the way to the sea is still not understood.) Offa's Dyke is still impressive and it needs little imagination to visualize what it must have symbolized twelve hundred years ago. But, of course, any ideas that these dykes were more than token defences is probably erroneous. They marked boundaries and they marked them in a convincing way. Nobody crossing Offa's Dyke could be under any illusion that he was in his own territory.

Precisely the same consideration applied to Wansdyke. The Wansdyke is an impressive fortification which extends from Portishead in the Bristol Channel to the Inkpen Beacon in Berkshire – a distance of sixty miles. It consists of a bank with a ditch to the north side. The bank is high enough and the ditch deep enough to be a considerable obstacle to an attacking army, though its delaying effect would be only temporary. The Wansdyke runs through farms and private property. The author found no difficulty inspecting it but was informed by landowners that car-drivers are regarded with some suspicion unless they have asked and been granted permission to cross land. This attitude does not stem from unfriendliness but has a more serious cause. A growing menace is cattle- and sheep-stealing from large farms. The procedure is that a car-driver makes a reconnaissance by day – but takes good care not to approach anyone who might note the car number. At night a lorry will follow the car-driver's directions and steal – perhaps slaughtering on the spot – valuable livestock. The innocent battlefield visitor may thus be regarded with suspicion unless he declares his identity and intent. In most places it is not necessary, but where roads are marked 'private' it is. It is very rare indeed for a farmer to object to a visit by a genuine archaeologist or student of military history.

The visitor will notice that dykes are often broken, and the height of the rampart also varies from place to place. In the eastern section of the Wansdyke the bank is approximately fifteen feet high; in the western sector it is approximately four feet. Broken sections, i.e. places where the dyke has not been built, are accounted for by the former presence of other long-vanished defences – a densely-tangled thicket perhaps, or a marsh. It is necessary to look for possible traces of such features in sectors where battles took place, for such obstacles would have determined the path of armies. Nowadays most roads have been straightened, but over the country there are still places where a road wanders back and forth in a zigzag across apparently flat, featureless country. Perhaps in former times it was the track over a marsh, with fallen trees, standing trees, or a pool diverting it first one way and then another.

We know very little about Wansdyke, which may or may not have once been called Wodensdyke. The man responsible for its construction was probably Egbert who became king of Wessex in the year 800, but it may have been started by his predecessor Kenulf. Some writers have contended that it was built by the Mercians but this theory is, to put it mildly, unlikely, as the ditch faces the wrong way for their purposes. The great Offa had died in 794 and his successors were less statesmen than warlike predators. Two years after Offa's death the new king of Mercia raided Kent, captured its king, cut off his hands and blinded him. The Wansdyke might not stop an army but it would stop lightning raids of this type if properly patrolled. Egbert was no mean warrior himself. In 815 he was reported as ravaging Cornwall from east to west; if he went this distance from his base he would need some sort of defensive line between his own kingdom and the turbulent Mercians.

Beornwulf, who was defeated at the Battle of Ellandun in 825, seems to have become King of Mercia by a *coup d'état* the previous year. Like all usurpers who obtained the throne by an adroit move he needed to give his army something to do and something to think about, as well as some rewards, lest they should look upon their new ruler with too critical an eye. There was, of course, every chance of being toppled off his throne by an incursion from Wessex. Beornwulf therefore decided on a pre-emptive strike. He probably moved east as if to attack a target in south-eastern England and then doubled back and came racing down the Berkshire Ridgeway. At Overton he would twist again, leaving the Ridgeway, and having made a survey from the superb observation point at Silbury Hill would then come up the track by All Cannings Down. On the way he would encounter other defensive earthworks, for this was clearly considered to be a vulnerable spot. It is a confusing area to identify, for the 2½-inch map which was last fully revised in 1921, and has been only partly revised since, does not bear many of the features the visitor will find; equally it makes very plain some he will find difficult to discern. Allington itself is on the other side of the Wansdyke and thus far removed from the battlefield; he must also ignore All Cannings, interesting though this is. The best route to the battlefield is from Beckhampton north of the Wansdyke, which will bring him between Allington Down and All Cannings Down. Here on the forward slopes we believe that the Battle of Ellandun was fought.

This opinion is based less on the similarity between the names of Ellandun and Allington than on the probable strategy of Beornwulf. Beornwulf was no novice at the art of war; whatever qualities he might have lacked, tactical appreciation would not be among them. He would know very well that if he made his approach to the Wansdyke obvious a suitable reception would be there to greet him. He would therefore wish to achieve one of the first principles of war – deception of the enemy – and having come down the Ridgeway rapidly, possibly with the advantage of surprise, he would then send a small party ahead to suggest that he was marching by the quickest possible route to Salisbury. At that point Ecgbert would throw everything in his way, he hoped, but Beornwulf by a swift change of direction would be over the Wansdyke and on Ecgbert's flank, if not actually behind him.

What went wrong? Why did Ecgbert gain victory and why was it, as the *Anglo-Saxon Chronicle* puts it, 'a great slaughter was made there'?

Undoubtedly Ecgbert was the more experienced general. He had been on the throne for many years and had fought a number of successful campaigns against the Britons. It is unlikely that he would not have had spies and scouts in Mercia, and even some perhaps in circles very close to Beornwulf's councils. And, as a good soldier, he would believe in winning his battles before he fought them. Winning this battle would mean preparing all possible approach routes so that an invading army would have already encountered much resistance before it reached the Wansdyke. The ground at Allington looks highly dangerous, with forward earthworks, flanking slopes, deceptive hollows, and an enclosed arena. Once among those slopes Beornwulf's army would have little room for manœuvre in any sense of the word. One visualizes his army trapped between the two sets of earthworks, desperately trying to force its way up to the Wansdyke and break through, harassed by flank attacks, and unable to retreat and regroup without being disrupted. It was, it must be remembered, Saxon against Saxon, the same weapons, the same techniques, the same dogged courage. Both armies would have learnt something from their forays against the Britons, and both probably had Cornish or Welsh in their ranks as bowmen or spearmen. The West Saxons would have some advantage from the fact that they were uphill to the Mercians; in all battles where hand-thrown missiles – spears, axes, or darts, or even arrows – were used the men on the upper slope had a slight but vital margin of range. Missiles could be flighted to carry farther from a height. The reader may test this by taking a javelin and throwing it first uphill and then down. The difference in range may be a surprise, as perhaps it was to the Mercians in 825. An oncoming spear (or javelin) is difficult to judge and always pitches closer to you than you anticipated, as many an unwary spectator of a javelin-throwing event has experienced. Spear-throwers who charge downhill have the advantage of range and impetus, and if their spears fail to find targets they may be recovered. The spearman charging uphill is in a vastly inferior position. Beornwulf having put his men into that disadvantageous attack would not be able to recover them and prevent their slaughter. Like many brilliant tactical moves his rapid feint and change of direction deserved success. Unfortunately for his army he met an even shrewder tactician and 'there was a great slaughter'. It was not the end of Beornwulf, for he escaped from the field and turned his attention to East Anglia, where he was killed later in the year. It was, however, the end of Mercian paramountcy. Four years later Ecgbert took a great army into Mercia and carried all before him as far as the Humber. The Northumbrians fought back but were decisively defeated at Dore, and acknowledged Ecgbert as Bretwalda. The following year he was conducting a successful campaign against the Welsh.

He was not always successful. There was a new and formidable threat on the English scene. In 787 three Viking ships had arrived in Dorset, landed their crews, and ravaged the country. By the time of Ecgbert's reign the Vikings were a continuous threat. In 836 he lost a battle to them, although two years later he won an even larger one against a combined force of Vikings and Welsh at Hingston Down near Plymouth. By that time something was known of these relentless northern warriors. They were called Danes but many of them came from other countries. At this stage Ecgbert was the only English king to put up much of a defence against them, and after his death in 839 England sank steadily into decline.

Ecgbert was a remarkable king. He reigned for thirty-seven years and was the ancestor of all subsequent monarchs of England, save four. His early life had been spent in exile, some of it at the court of Charlemagne, and he would never have obtained the throne at all if a cousin had not died prematurely.

By the time of Ecgbert's reign the Saxons were a very different people from those we described earlier in the book. They were Christian and in many ways cultured and civilized. They had established settlements by clearing forests, and often named them after the local chief, as in Wolverton (Wulfhere's tun – 'tun' meaning a village). 'Ham' meant home, and Birmingham was the home of Beormund's people. Many English place-names have English origins, but this is a large and complicated subject which concerns us here only in that it occasionally gives some guidance to the sites and approach roads of battlefields.

Before leaving Ellandun we might look at sites which other writers have suggested. Wroughton, immediately south of Swindon, has been suggested, and so has Lydiard Tregoze, just to the west. Amesbury has also had its supporters. However, at none of these places is there any reason why they should have been chosen for a major battle in contrast to Allington which is in exactly the right place for the strategic and tactical situation of the time.

THE BATTLE OF ASHDOWN

AD 871

The early years of the ninth century saw a bloody and disastrous succession of battles against the new invaders. Apart from bare dates we have no details of these encounters, for the Vikings usually won and there were seldom survivors. The Vikings were terrible adversaries. Opinion is divided whether the word 'Viking' comes from 'Wicing', meaning warrior, or from 'Wic', the creek by which they penetrated far inland in their shallow-draught boats. They were hated by the Saxons, who had now settled into being a Christian, agricultural community, and their cruelty, destruction and heathenism caused them to be branded as uncivilized barbarians; however, in recent years, archaeological discoveries have established that the Vikings had a well-developed culture of their own.

But to the Saxons they were an appalling problem. In their long, graceful boats they could range far and wide, for if the wind failed all would take a turn on the oars, and it was not unusual for them to cover 200 miles in twenty-four hours. On land they would often appropriate horses, of which there were many in East Anglia, and thus widen the range of their raiding. When they were victorious they sacked and burned towns and churches, monasteries and villages; if by any chance they encountered strong resistance they would move on and carry their brand of destruction elsewhere where they were not expected. Capturing their leaders availed nothing for these were merely local chiefs who were useless as hostages. And the complete disregard they had for the lives of their opponents was matched by their attitude to their own. In a storm they would drive their boats at top speed, glorying in the savagery and danger of it all, often letting them smash on the rocks because they would not trouble to shorten sail. Small wonder that the Saxons soon included in the Christian services the words 'From the fury of the Norsemen, good Lord deliver us' (*A furore Normanorum libera nos*). Curiously enough some of these Norsemen were to settle in France, become known as the Normans (in English as well as Latin), and develop the motte and bailey castle which was the military answer to their own type of raiding.

As the news of the vulnerability of England travelled back to Scandinavia and the adjoining countries, raids became more continuous and were made by larger bodies of men. Soon too the Vikings, who were short of land in their own country, began to settle. This new and ominous trend drew Saxon attention away from their own fratricidal squabbles. In 841 we read that:

In this year Ealdorman Hercbehrt was killed by heathen men and many men with him in the marsh and later in the same year many were killed in Lindsay, East Anglia, and Kent.

In 842 many were killed in London and Rochester.

In 843 King Aethulwulf fought against the crews of 35 ships at Carhampton, and the Danes had possession of the battlefield.

Whether called Danes, Vikings or Norsemen made no difference, but usually they were known as Danes, as, we will call them from now on.

In 845 the people of Somerset and the people of Dorset fought against the Danish army at the mouth of the Parret and there made a great slaughter and had the victory.

The only salvation apparently was in unity, difficult though it might be for the Saxons to achieve.

In 851, we read:

In this year the men of Devon fought against the heathen army at Wicgeanburg and the English made great slaughter there and had the victory. And the same year 350 ships came into the mouth of the Thames and stormed Canterbury and London and put to flight Brihtwulf, King of the Mercians, with his army, and went south across the Thames into Surrey. And King Aethelwulf and his son Aethelbald fought against them at Aclea with the army of the West Saxons and there inflicted the greatest slaughter that we ever heard of until this present day, and had the victory there.

Aethelwulf had presumably learnt something from his previous defeat, and now had won a victory. Unfortunately it was not enough. The Danes were filtering through in all directions. Some had fortified themselves in Thanet and Sheppey and could not be driven out. In desperation the West Saxons deposed Aethelwulf and elected his son in his place. But events became no better. The Danes even burnt Winchester, the capital of Wessex, and sacked York. Northumbria was occupied by them and reverted to barbarism; those inhabitants of Yorkshire who were not killed were made serfs. The northern thrust had been made by the 'Great Army', under two Kings, Guthrum and Bagsaeg, but even after its northern conquest it was still land-hungry. One section went off to East Anglia where it fought King Edmund. Edmund was a rare combination, efficient, saintly, and a good military leader, but these qualities did not bring him victory against the Danes. He was taken prisoner, and tortured to make him worship Danish gods. He refused and was used as target practice for bowmen. His body was recovered and buried in what became the Abbey of Bury St Edmunds. The Danes then proceeded to divide East Anglia among themselves.

It was now the turn of Wessex. After Aethelwulf's deposition his three elder sons, Aethelbald, Aethelbert and Aethelred, ruled in succession. In 870 when the 'Great Army' sailed up the Thames and launched itself into Wessex, Aethelred came out to meet them, aided by his eighteen-year-old brother, Alfred. Aethelred's contribution tends to be overlooked in comparison with that of his younger brother but this is neither accurate nor just. Brilliant though Alfred was, he would have had no chance to display his abilities had not Aethelred been almost equally capable.

Alfred would, of course, have been exceptional in any age and was a giant in his time. As a child he had been sent to Rome to be baptized by Pope Leo. From early youth he had shown great promise as a scholar, and had been given that special type of leadership which brings out the best in men whatever their abilities and interests. Vitally important at that time was his military ability. He was an inspiring figure on the battlefield but he knew – as all good generals do – that there is a lot more to winning a war than a single victory. In those days – and perhaps up to the present century – boys took to war as naturally as they do to football or boxing today. And just as many a modern lad practises football in every spare moment he has, dreaming of a great opportunity against another country so did Saxon lads, particularly those of royal blood, practise for war. Thus when the Danes moved into Mercia and took up winter quarters at Nottingham, Burgred, King of Mercia, appealed to Aethelred and Alfred to help him. Alfred was sixteen at the time but a veteran of many battles and skirmishes.

By this time the Danes were a large organized force. This conferred disadvantages as well as advantages. The old style small raiding forces could live off the country, had no disciplinary problems, needed few orders, and did not need to hold ground. This new army had a logistical problem; it needed to be near food supplies, it needed space to deploy, and it needed a unified command. Furthermore it was not operating against unprepared and helpless monks or villages; it was confronted with an armed countryside, full of look-outs, a place where food would be difficult to obtain and where stragglers or small foraging parties would be cut off and exterminated. It had lost surprise and it had lost much of its mobility. It could indeed send raiders on horseback for isolated forays but the mass of the army was bound to be slow-moving and cumbersome. Alfred would have noted that.

Like the Saxons, the Danes fought with swords sometimes, but their favourite weapon was the battle-axe. It was a two-handed weapon and in the hands of the right man it could be used adroitly for thrusting and parrying. Nevertheless, although the axe was a far more versatile weapon than is usually believed, it carried one considerable disadvantage. It needed space. It could not be brought into action rapidly in a surprise attack unless the attacked men were in open order (widely separated) and, if they were in open order, it would be that little easier to split a way through them, whirling axes notwithstanding. There is, of course, a peculiar fascination about a weapon which is swung, whether it is axe, sword, or rifle butt, but there is often an excellent chance that it may do more damage to your friends than your foes, as your own side are likely to be closer to you. And although it could be used as a spear it was a poor substitute. All this Alfred would have noted when he went to help the Mercians at Nottingham, and fought a drawn battle with the Danes. It was a man's weapon, the axe, and the Danes loved it; they could slice an enemy in half with an axe, and literally carve a path to victory. Soldiers are very conservative about weapons, and sentiment about them often blinds them to the need for change. 'I would like to see the machine-gun that could stop one of my cavalry charges,' a pre-1914 officer once said – and a year later he did. The battle-axe, even after it had failed to save the Saxons at Hastings, and was discredited as a weapon, still managed to worm its way back into favour with the Normans, and in the twelfth century was Richard the Lion Heart's favourite weapon.

The Danes, flushed with their East Anglian and other successes, set up headquarters at Reading. They realized that they had not yet met the full power of Saxon resistance and that it would be concentrated somewhere in this area. Apart from anything else, they would be outnumbered, and they were experienced enough to know that a disparity in numbers can be nullified if the lesser force fights behind defences – or at least from prepared positions. There are, of course, other factors which can equalize numbers: weapons, experience, training, and tactical handling, but the most consistent is fortifications. Surprisingly perhaps, they made a rampart between the rivers Thames and Kennet on the right side of the royal city. We have two different accounts of the subsequent events, one from the *Anglo-Saxon Chronicle*, the other from Asser, Bishop of Sherborne and a contemporary of Alfred.

While some of the Danes were making the defences others 'scoured the country for plunder'. They were soon proved right in their expectations of resistance for:

> They were encountered by Ethelwulf, the ealdorman of Berkshire, at a place called Englefield, both sides fought bravely and made long resistance. At length one of the pagan jarls was slain, and the greater part of the army destroyed; upon which the rest saved themselves by flight, and the Christians gained the victory.
>
> Four days afterwards, Aethelred, King of the West Saxons, and his brother, Alfred, united their forces and marched to Reading, where, on their arrival, they cut to pieces the pagans whom they found outside the fortifications. But the pagans, nevertheless, sallied out from the gates and a long and fierce engagement ensued. At last, grief to say, the Christians fled, the pagans obtained the victory, and the aforesaid ealdorman Ethelwulf [victor of Englefield] was among the slain. (*Asser*)

It was a disaster for the West Saxons and the Danes realized it. They themselves had sent out strong reconnaissance parties which had been beaten. The Saxons, overconfident perhaps, had thereupon attacked the Danes in their new stronghold and after bitter fighting had been cut to pieces. The Danes had not planned such a clever strategy in that they had drawn the Saxons to fight in a disadvantageous position but once it had happened they had taken full advantage of it. Now was the time to follow up the victory and carve Wessex in half. Four days later – a day to rest and to bury the dead, a day to regroup, a day to confer and

get ready, and on the march on the fourth, if not earlier —
they would have covered the ten miles from Reading to
Streatley and come up the long slope to the Ridgeway. No
doubt they kept a wary eye to the right as they went diagonally
up the track, and perhaps had a few look-outs along the sky-
line. But nothing happened and they would have concluded
that the Saxon morale had been destroyed at the barricades
and there would be no more resistance in that part of the
country. Once on top of the Ridge they were safe from surprise
attack; doubtless the Saxons would now keep well out of their
way.

But the Saxons were there, hundreds of them. Chroniclers
have a loose way of describing an army or the dead after a
battle as 'thousands'. It is doubtful if either side numbered
more than a thousand on this occasion, for the Danes would
have left some men to protect their base and the Saxons
would have found it difficult to concentrate their forces until
they knew exactly when and where the Danes would move.
And even today you could conceal a thousand men along the
Ridgeway, all ready to spring out and ambush the unwary.
In those days they could have laid up within weapon reach.
Some undoubtedly did but the main force was held in reserve
for the shock attack.

Alfred's problem was to manœuvre this invasion column
into a trap. It was no good fighting in a head-on clash along
the Ridgeway. The Danes were hard men to beat at the best
of times and in a straightforward fight were as likely as not
to come out the winners as they had, he knew only too well,
at Reading. The need was to lure them to a position where
they would be too cramped to make full use of their weapons.
It would not be easy. His army was there along the Ridgeway
by Roden Downs. Just north of the Ridgeway and south of
Lowbury Hill, site of the old Romano-British temple, was a
superb battlefield, like a parade ground, if that was what you
wanted. It is an open piece of slightly hollow ground, and
it still has a thorn tree in the middle of it. The Danes would
like that: it would give them room to swing their axes.

Alfred drew them towards it by a decoy party. This, the

Danes thought, when they caught sight of them, was the rest of the Saxon army. They moved forward to cut them to pieces, but the Saxons fell back. The Danes were in two divisions, and it was very necessary for the Saxons to decoy them all into the right position before they launched their attack. If the Saxons went in too soon the Danish rear party would come in behind and they too would be trapped. And that was not Alfred's plan at all.

As they deployed on the battlefield which had been chosen for them, the Danes suddenly noticed that the main Saxon force was not in front of them but had suddenly appeared from behind them, cutting off their retreat. They suspected that they were the object of a tactical plan and they hastily re-formed, putting their two Kings in the middle, and positioning the jarls and lesser chiefs on the front and flanks. They put stakes in the ground, as this was the tried way of holding up an enemy charge; then they waited for the next Saxon move. The Saxons came forward and also put down stakes against a possible Danish charge. They too divided their army into two groups, but this was because Aethelred was not yet at the field. He was busy praying in his tent, and would not leave it. He took so long over his devotions that the Danes had begun the battle before he arrived. Alfred was in a desperate position, for without Aethelred's division he had not enough men for the tactical thrust he had planned. Asser put it:

The Alfred, though possessing a subordinate authority, could no longer support the troops of the enemy unless he retreated or charged upon them without waiting for his brother. At length he bravely led his troops against the hostile army, as they had before arranged, but without waiting for his brother's arrival; for he relied on the divine counsels, and forming his men into a dense phalanx, marched on at once to meet the foe.

What Alfred knew, and the Danes as yet did not, was that to the east of Lowbury Hill, and behind the Danish position, was a precipice falling to what is now known (and marked on the map) as Dean's Bottom. 'Denu' is the old English word for a dene or valley, but 'dene' can also derive from Dane. As Danish weapons have been found at the bottom of this valley it seems as if at least a part of Alfred's plan worked. Driving with tremendous force on to the Danish lines he made them fall back to give themselves more room. The Saxon casualties would have been very high as they charged up the slopes on to an army which was prepared to receive them. Only superb leadership could have taken that Saxon force to the point at which the retreating Danes, unfamiliar with the countryside, would find a precipice behind them, if they were not already over it. The visitor will do well to be careful or he might share their experience. And as the rear line steadied and came forward involuntarily the swinging axes would do as much harm to their own side as to the Saxons. Something like panic would infect the Danes for there are few more unnerving experiences than trying to confront an enemy who is trying to push you over a precipice which lies just behind you and which you dare not turn round to look for. At that point, Aethelred's men, heartened by the successful conclusion of his prayers, hurled themselves into the battle. To the Danes it looked as if fresh tides of reinforcements were on the way. Some tried to fight their way out sideways but Alfred's flankers took care of that and shepherded them on to the deadly slopes.

And when both armies had fought long and bravely, at last the pagans, by the divine judgement, were no longer able to bear the attacks of the Christians, and having lost the greater part of their army, took to disgraceful flight. One of their two kings, and five jarls, were there slain, together with many thousand pagans, who fell on all sides, covering with their bodies the whole plain of Ashdune.

There fell in that battle King Bagsac, jarl Sidrac the elder, and jarl Sidrac the younger, jarl Osbern, jarl Frene, and jarl Harald, and the whole pagan army pursued its flight, not only until evening but until the next day, until they reached the stronghold from which they had sallied. The Christians followed, slaying all they could reach, until it became dark.

The *Anglo-Saxon Chronicle* records the death of two kings, not one, and the same number of earls. It says 'many thousands were killed and they continued fighting until night'. And, as on many battlefields, you may still perhaps hear and even see the fighting, in the morning mists at certain times of the year. Imagination, no doubt, and self-deception, but real enough to those who claim to have seen it re-enacted in ghostly but frightening reincarnation.

THE BATTLE OF ETHANDUN

AD 878

Ashdown, although a great victory, had merely checked the Danes, not ended their campaign. Alfred's efforts to follow it up, and drive the Danes out of Wessex, met with very moderate success. Two weeks after Ashdown, he fought another Danish army at Basing, near Basingstoke, and there – the *Chronicle* bluntly and briefly reports – 'the Danes had the victory'.

And two months later, King Aethelred and his brother Alfred fought against the army at Merton, and they were in two divisions; and they put both to flight, and were victorious far on into the day, and there was great slaughter on both sides, and the Danes had possession of the battle-field. And after this battle a great summer army came to Reading.

Clearly there is some characteristic in these Danish armies which the chronicler omits, perhaps because he does not know it or perhaps because he does not understand it. Why did the Danes win these battles? Presumably it was not merely a matter of numbers. Both sides had enormous casualties. Why at Merton did they put the Danes to flight and yet lose? Were the Danes experts at luring their opponents on to destruction, perhaps in a series of enveloping moves? All in all it suggests that there was much more subtlety in these battles than a mere rabble of spear-throwers meeting a collection of battle-axe swingers in a head-on clash. It looks as if the Danes were capable of fighting delaying actions and then committing reserves at the critical moment.

There is of course another explanation, and that is that Alfred knew when to break off his engagements. Alfred was a highly intelligent general who underrated neither his enemies nor his task. The war was one of constant mobility. Alfred was, doubtless, constantly harassing and diverting the Danish invaders. Occasionally his strategy brought him to a pitched battle. The time and place were probably of his choosing, although there were doubtless occasions when he made a mistake and the Danes held the initiative. The Danes should not have had superiority of numbers, for the population of England was probably 900,000 at that time; but Alfred may have known only too well that in a pitched battle the Danes were, man for man, better than the Saxons. It seems that Alfred used small groups to inflict hammer blows in hit-and-run tactics. Aethelred had died after the Battle of Merton, and Alfred, still very young, had to fight a war in which he did not dare commit all his forces. One great defeat and his kingdom was lost. At Wilton (near Salisbury), still in 871 – a year of battle if ever there was one – the Saxons took on a huge Danish army and put it to flight, but had to retreat hastily when the Danes rallied. The cost to both sides was punitive. The Saxons were fighting for their kingdom so, even though outnumbered and often outfought, they made the Danes respect them. Eventually, after heavy losses on both sides, a truce was signed at the end of the year 871.

The year 872 seems to have been a comparatively un-eventful period though there can be no doubt that it must have been full of minor clashes and skirmishes. By this time both armies had acquired a healthy respect for each other. The Danes knew that, until the Saxons were finally conquered and crushed, their own gains could not be regarded as secure. The Saxons – or at least Alfred – realized that the Danes might come up the Thames via Reading, might drive up from Portsmouth and Southampton by Winchester, or might even swoop down from Northumbria through Mercia. Faced with this triple-pronged threat he had to evolve a strategy which would defeat these relentless heathen savages. In 873 the Danes busied themselves in Northumbria, but they also established a strong base in Lindsay. In 874 they moved across to Repton in Derbyshire, conquered the Mercian kingdom, and installed a puppet king there.

In 875 they were up in the north again, based on the Tyne and ranging far and wide and into Scotland. Guthrum and two lesser chieftains moved to Cambridge. For the time being the Danes seemed to have abandoned their efforts to split Wessex in two by advancing from Reading. Doubtless they knew that preparations had been made for them along the Ridgeway and other trackways. By this time Alfred had Wessex very well organized militarily and was an expert at lightning commando-type raids. It was the Danes' own technique, but they themselves were particularly vulnerable to it. Alfred carried the war to them by sea. In 875 he engaged seven Danish ships, captured one, and put the rest to flight. He was, very rightly, determined not to let his enemies settle down. This phase of the war became a vicious deadlock with plenty of activity but no thrustful moves.

Suddenly the Danes broke it. The Cambridge army slipped away south and west, and next appeared at Wareham in Dorset. One large contingent had marched to the coast, embarked, and come round by sea: the ultimate effect was that a huge Danish force had outflanked the Wessex army and was now posing a threat from the rear. Many in this force seem to have been mounted, although they would not have contemplated fighting from horseback, horses being regarded merely as personnel carriers.

Alfred seems to have moved almost as swiftly and he had the advantage that he was operating from interior lines. He swept down to Dorset and had the Danes boxed in before they realized what had happened. Instead of being able to forage and settle in, they were trapped. Possibly Alfred had his navy behind them at sea. At all events they decided to ask for terms and even gave him hostages of high rank. Furthermore, they swore on the 'holy ring', a most sacred Icelandic symbol, that they would promptly leave England. Their humiliation was complete. Their great strategic enveloping move had trapped no one but themselves. Alfred trusted them; they could not possibly break so important an oath. But they did. Under cover of darkness they mounted their horses and slipped away to Exeter. Some had embarked and were making the dash by sea but these ran into a storm and it is reported in the *Anglo-Saxon Chronicle* that 120 ships were lost at Swanage. When he heard the news of the Danes' treachery, Alfred cursed himself for trusting them but wasted no time in setting off in rapid pursuit. Unfortunately for him, his enemies had had too much start and were safely in the fortress before he could intercept them. There again they asked for terms.

The battle of wits had lost none of its sharpness. As Alfred knew, and the Danes also knew, he could not afford to keep his army besieging them in Exeter. If the Danes' supplies began to run low they could be revictualled from ships. They would not, in any event, have to hold out for long. Armies at this period, and for a thousand years later, had a limited campaigning season because every able-bodied man was needed for the spring sowing and again the autumn reaping. During the bad weather all armies stayed in winter quarters; campaigning in wet, snow, mud and short days was too hazardous to be embarked on voluntarily. At Exeter the Danes knew that if Alfred did not break in immediately his men must withdraw to get in the harvest which was now due. If they did not, his army and kingdom would probably starve, and their fighting qualities next summer after a winter of exceptional and unnecessary deprivation would be negligible. To help Alfred make up his mind, the Danes offered even more hostages, so many in fact that he could not fail to accept their offer. And this time they kept to the terms he gave them, more or less. Some returned to Mercia and others went to Gloucester but they did no more fighting. It is unlikely that Alfred trusted them but he felt that for the time being they were under control. He was wrong.

This campaign of Saxons against Danes, or more particularly of Alfred against an unknown Danish strategist, is one of which we have tantalizingly few details. This winter (877–8) the Danes broke all the military rules. Instead of lying up for the winter months, preparing their weapons, quarrelling and drinking, they began a new campaign. On 6 January 878 or thereabouts, they slipped quietly up to Chippenham, set up a battle headquarters, and launched a series of lightning attacks far and wide on the astonished Saxons. Where they had come from no one precisely knew, probably from Bristol, with reinforcements which had slipped down from Mercia. Surprise, speed and ruthlessness drove all before them and soon Alfred, with his command scattered and distintegrated, was a homeless fugitive. The best he could do was to take a small band of loyal adherents into the fens of Somerset. There they dispersed for secrecy and safety. But the Danes were not having matters all their own way for it was reported that an attempt to invade Devon with twenty-three ships, was decisively defeated. Whether this Saxon army was led by Alfred or not is not known.

Possibly 878 was a mild and dry winter. Whatever the weather and conditions, neither side allowed them to affect plans. From his secure retreat Alfred issued instructions for the mobilizing of his army. It took weeks. The Danes found out where he was and tried to attack him but attacking an enemy who is hiding in the fens and has local guides is a frustrating task. As often as not your own army will be decoyed into treacherous bogs or ambushed where it is unable to escape. Alfred was fighting for survival. Whether the legends of the burnt cakes, or his creeping into the Danish camp disguised as a minstrel to hear their plan are true or not is immaterial. They could well have been. He was desperate, and he needed to know something of the Danish dispositions. When he eventually moved out in May 878 he was joined by a host of men who had all been summoned to meet him. This was a carefully planned and timed operation. Then he set out to meet the Danes.

The place where he met them and won a decisive battle has been a matter of some controversy. The name Ethandun has been taken to mean Heddington in Wiltshire, which is not improbable, Eddington and Yattendon in Berkshire, which are highly unlikely, Edington in Somerset, and Edington in Wiltshire. The last is the one we favour.

If opinions on the whereabouts of the battle-site vary so, no less do views of how the battle was fought even among those who prefer the Edington (Wilts) site. Some of these views appear to us to be unnecessarily complicated. The obvious inference is that the Danes, having heard that Alfred had broken out of Somerset, and somehow assembled an army, would immediately set out to crush this possible danger before it could rally too many forces and perhaps capture various strategic points. Their main headquarters was still at Chippenham and they would head south-west rapidly towards Somerset. Fourteen miles south of Chippenham they would come on to the B.3098 and turn towards Westbury. They would not at this stage expect to be anywhere near the Saxons. Alfred already knew that surprise is a war-winning factor, and in the last round of battles had been surprised himself – with disastrous results. Doubtless he sent some misinformation to the Danes, and made sure they had no idea of the trap he was laying for them. Where the B.3098 runs along the side of Edington Hill the visitor will note that some of the slopes are covered with woods and bracken. In 878 all the slopes would have been covered. They would be leafy and opaque. It was a perfect ambush position. If matters went badly, and the Danes had too many troops, the Saxons could retreat up the hill and perhaps occupy the hill fort known as Bratton Castle or even go right back to Battlesbury Camp. But they were not there to fight a defensive battle. Their total aim was to catch the whole Danish force unawares. Their numbers were obviously much greater than the Danes would expect, if the latter expected anything at all.

And the Danes, who would have been watched all the way till they reached the road, obligingly walked right into the trap. When their whole line of march was strung along that dangerous piece of road the Saxon attack would hurl itself on to them with all the pent-up rage and hate of men who have been living on the run in the woods for months. The *Chronicle* puts it briefly but clearly:

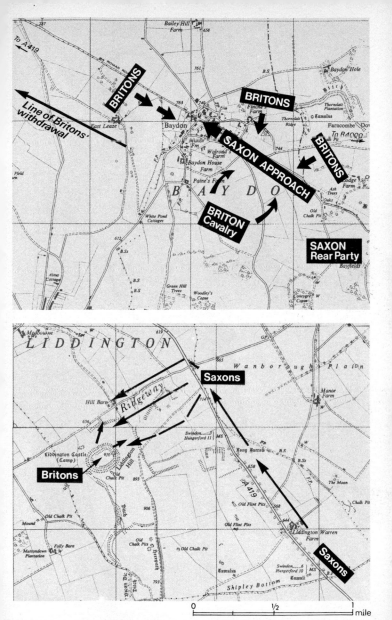

I Mount Badon, 516 *(Crown Copyright Reserved)*

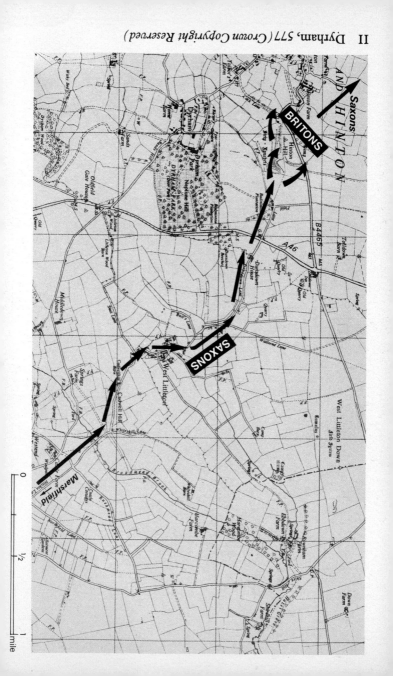

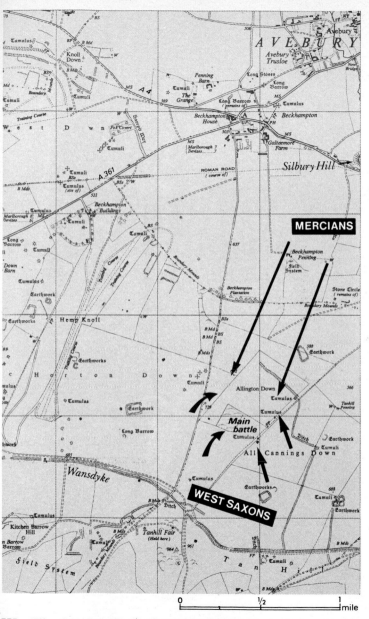

III   Ellandun, 825 *(Crown Copyright Reserved)*

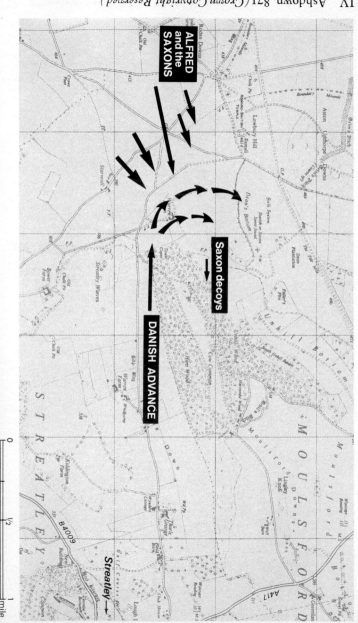

IV Ashdown, 871 (*Crown Copyright Reserved*)

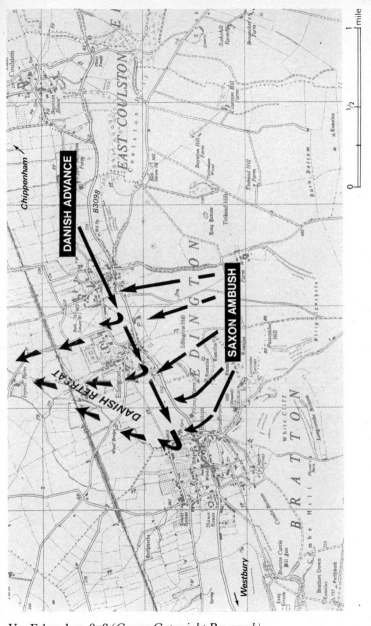

V Ethandun, 878 *(Crown Copyright Reserved)*

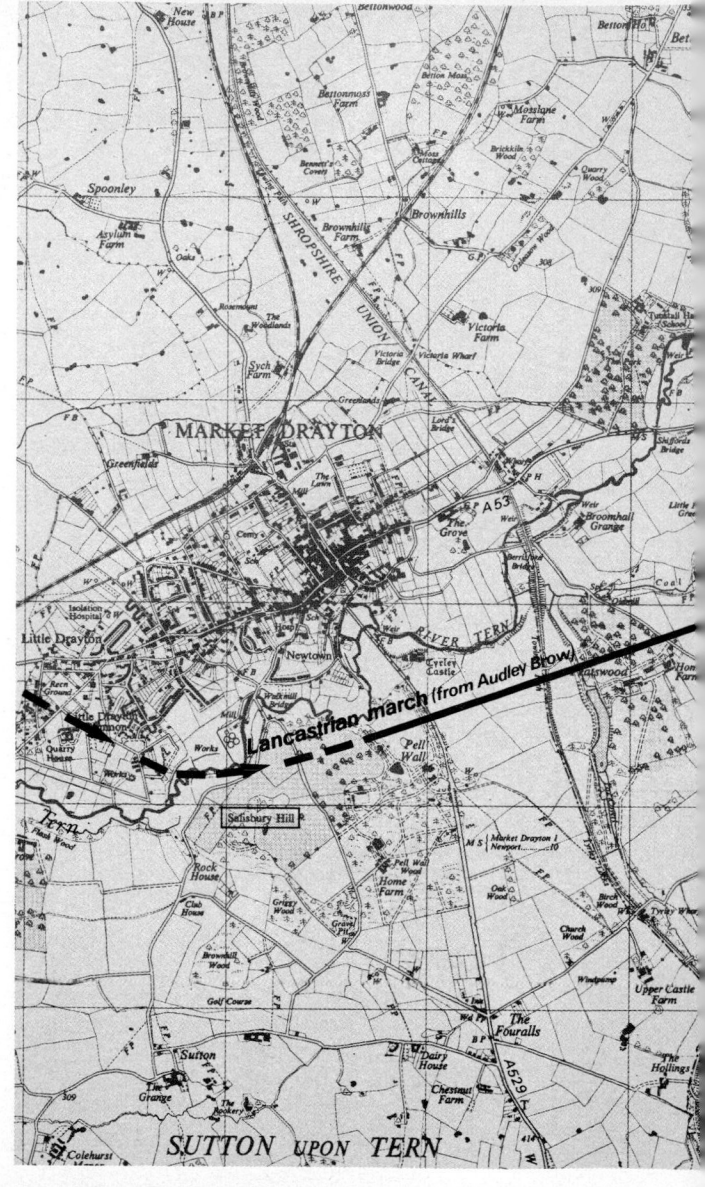

VI   Blore Heath, 1459 *(Crown Copyright Reserved)*

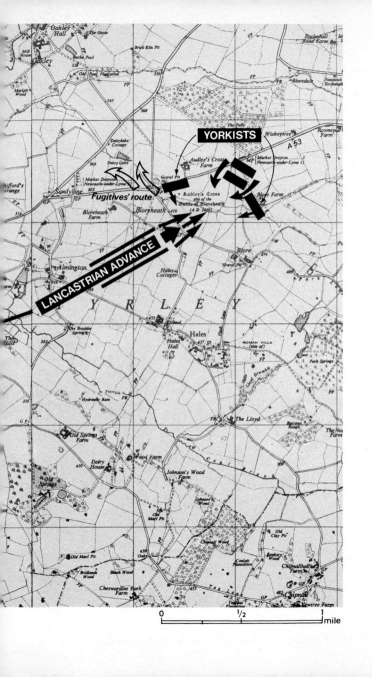

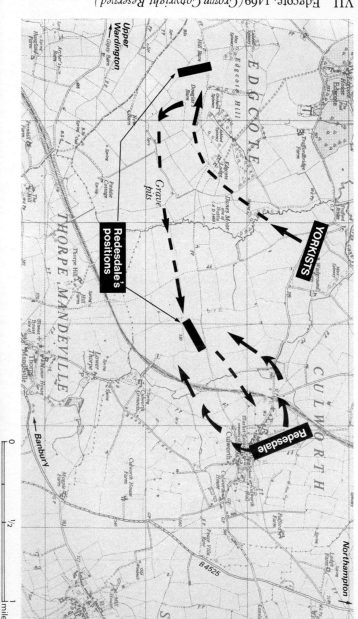

Upper
Wardington

EDGCOTE

Hill Barn

Douglas Barn

Grave
pits

Danes Moor
site of
2 Battle
(A.D.1469)

Redesdale's
positions

YORKISTS

THORPE MANDEVILLE

CULWORTH

Redesdale

Banbury

Northampton

0   ½   1
                 mile

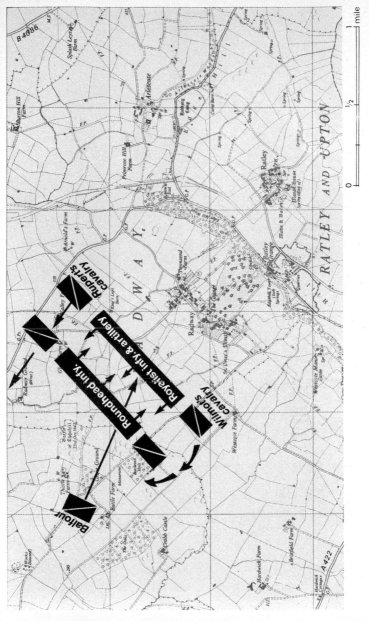

VIII   Edgehill, 1642 *(Crown Copyright Reserved)*

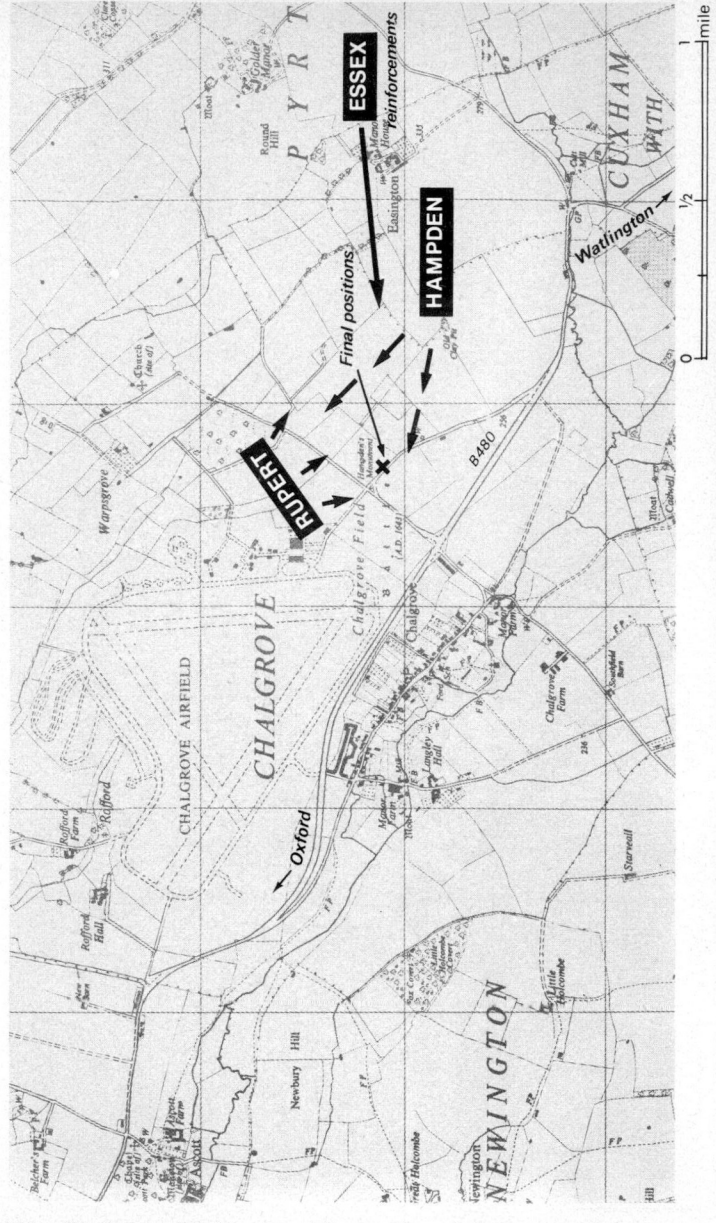

IX   Chalgrove Field, 1643 *(Crown Copyright Reserved)*

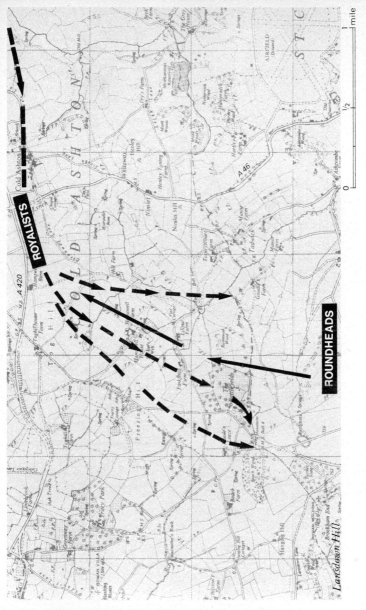

X Lansdown, 1643 *(Crown Copyright Reserved)*

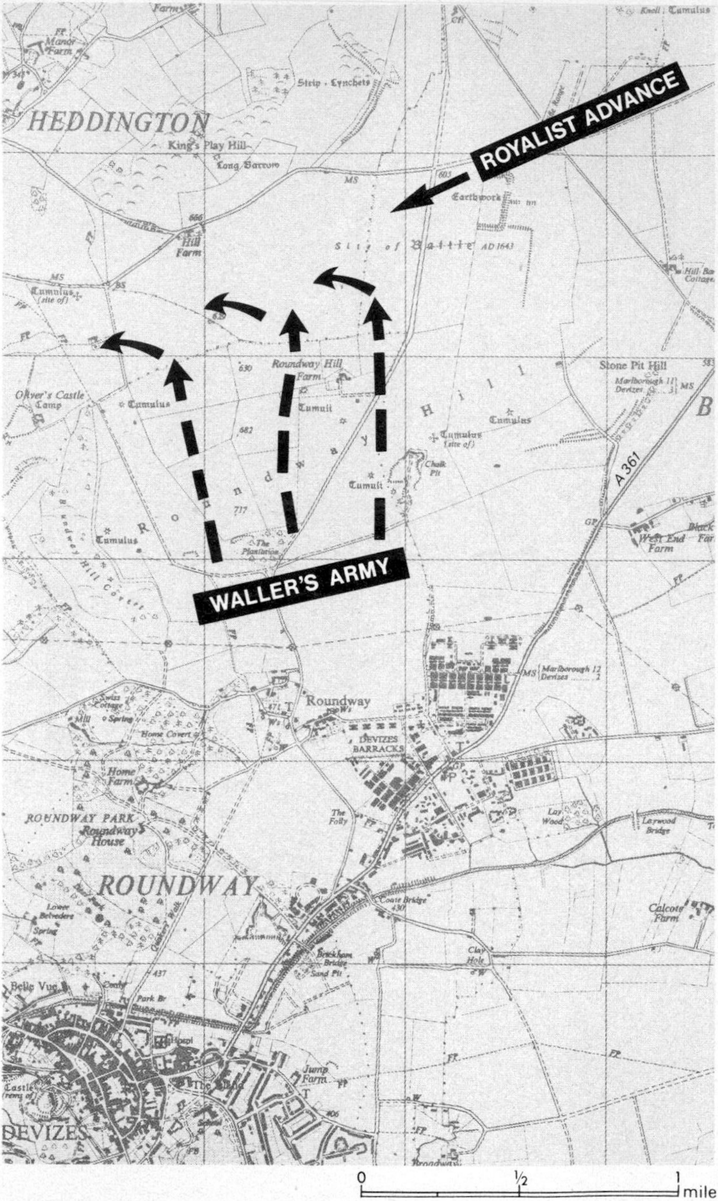

XI Roundway Down, 1643 *(Crown Copyright Reserved)*

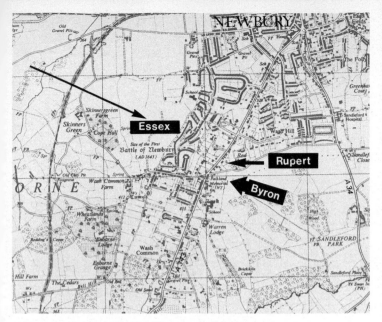

XII   Newbury, 1643 *(Crown Copyright Reserved)*

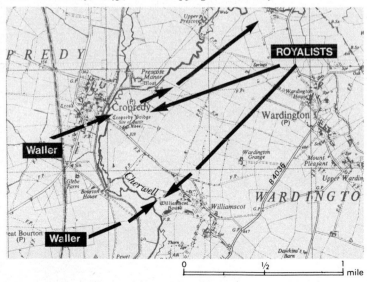

XIII   Cropredy Bridge, 1644 *(Crown Copyright Reserved)*

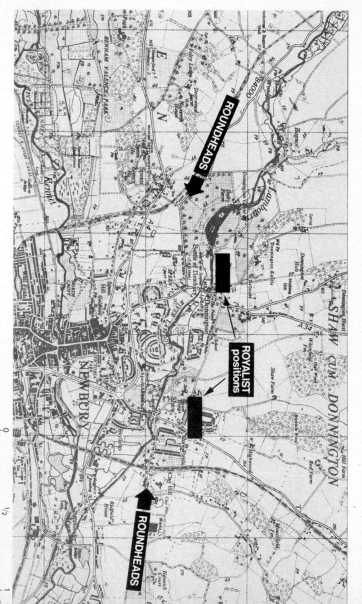

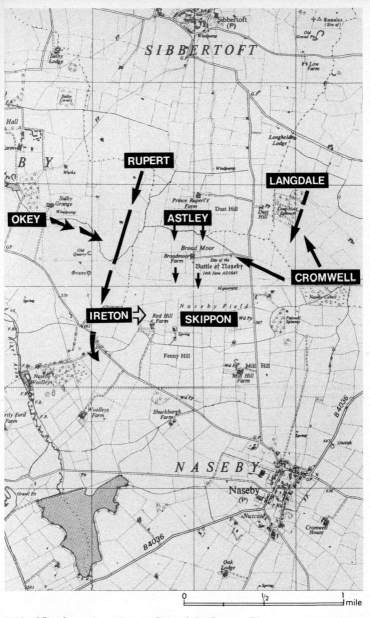

XV   Naseby, 1645 *(Crown Copyright Reserved)*

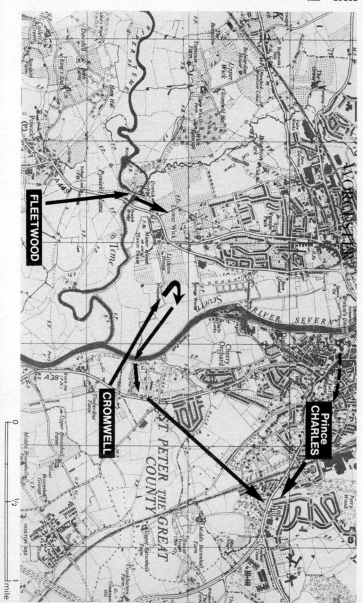

And there fought against the whole army and put it to flight, and pursued it as far as the fortress, and stayed there a fortnight.

Now indeed it was the Britons' turn. The Danes were so shocked, cut up and demoralized by this sudden and overwhelming defeat that they lost heart. It was, of course, a crushing blow to morale to have your great and victorious army destroyed by an enemy whom you thought you had yourself destroyed. The extraordinary aftermath of this battle was that Guthrum, the great Danish war leader, now decided that he had been following false gods and they had betrayed him. After the peace treaty, which this time was honoured, he was formally baptized. It was not, of course, the end of the Danish threat, for there were many different contingents, but the main force had been defeated and from then onwards Alfred saw his strength and authority increase. There was of course endless intermittent fighting, and some compromise, but the Anglo-Saxon kingdom had been saved, and the first steps to converting the Danes from paganism had already been taken.

Some writers have suggested that the main fighting took place south of Combe Hill. This implies that the Saxons would have fought uphill on to Danish prepared positions. Alfred would never have done anything so foolish, nor for that matter would the Danes, setting out to deal with what they thought to be an insurgent rabble fifty miles away, take up a defensive position on top of a barren ridge.

The visitor will have no difficulty in visualizing the ambush, the desperate fight, the Danes being tumbled down the slopes, and then the bitter pursuit to Chippenham.

THE BATTLE OF
BLORE HEATH

23 September 1459

The five hundred and eighty-one years which elapsed between the Battle of Ethandun and the Battle of Blore Heath were, of course, as eventful as any of those in our early history. However, many of the battles which occurred in them took place in areas covered by other books in this series, and certain of them, such as Evesham and Northampton, though geographically in the Midlands, were so closely linked with other battles, and so vital to the chain of events, that they were discussed in *British Battlefields: the South*. As far as possible an attempt has been made to preserve historical as well as geographical unity in this series. Nothing is more frustrating than to be standing on a battlefield well aware of what happened but completely baffled as to why it happened. Thus Lewes is so closely linked with Evesham that the latter is meaningless without the former. The events of the Wars of the Roses are extremely complex and the main sequence of battles falls outside this volume; however the two Midlands battles recorded here were apart from the main stream and are not closely linked with events before and after. When we reach the Civil War the converse applies and the main sequence appears in this volume.

The period between Ethandun and Blore Heath saw many developments, both in weapons and methods of warfare, but the main principles remained unchanged, as they still do. Thus numerical superiority may be offset by adequate defences, better tactics, or more efficient weapons; surprise confers great advantages, but if the initial advantage is not consolidated the success of the opening moves may have created dangerous liabilities which a cool and astute opponent may soon begin to exploit. The political pattern seemed to confirm the somewhat doubtful claim that history repeats itself. The Danes settled down just as their ferocious predecessors, the Anglo-Saxons, had done before them, and soon the blend of German and Scandinavian tribes became the loyal Englishmen who fought successfully at Stamford Bridge but unsuccessfully at Hastings.

The years immediately after the Norman Conquest did not see any major battles on English soil. Not until 1138 do we find what might be described as a representative army taking the field in this country. There were of course endless sieges, skirmishes and minor clashes before and after, but it is not until 1264 that we see the second great battle. (We might perhaps have to include Fornham in 1174 if we knew enough about it to determine its scale.) The year 1265 saw the decisive battle of Evesham, but then nearly a century elapsed before Boroughbridge in 1322. Neville's Cross took place in 1346, and Otterburn, over forty years later, in 1388. The early fifteenth century saw decisive and bloody battles at Homildon Hill in 1402 and Shrewsbury in 1403. There were, of course, numerous battles overseas in this long period. From Gerberoi (the occasion when William the Conqueror, fighting rebels led by Robert, his son, was wounded and unhorsed. Tokig of Wallingford, an English thegn, whose sister had married Robert d'Oilly, the builder of Oxford Castle, gave his own horse to William to make his escape, but was himself killed) in 1079, through Crécy, Poitiers, Agincourt, Beaugé, Formigny, and many others all over Europe, Englishmen were almost continuously in arms, sometimes for English causes, sometimes not, sometimes in victory, sometimes in defeat.

In 1455 at St Albans there began a long series of battles which only ended at Stoke Field, near Newark, in 1487. These were the infamous Wars of the Roses. Some hold that these wars ended with the Tewkesbury blood bath of 1471, but there were other battles still to come, not least that at Bosworth in 1485, before succession to the English throne was settled.

A very brief explanation of the Wars of the Roses is necessary here to give the background to the savage battle of Blore

Heath which we examine next.

The baronial war to which has been given the name 'Wars of the Roses' was not known by that name at the time, nor for many years afterwards. It was, however, fairly well represented by the White Rose of York against the Red Rose of Lancaster, in that a Lancastrian held the throne until he was driven from it by Yorkist supporters.

The root cause of the wars is held to be the will of Edward III who had distributed his realm so evenly that his descendants were equally and immensely powerful. Then, when his grandson, Richard II, ruled somewhat unwisely, he was toppled off his throne and undoubtedly murdered by his very rich cousin, Henry of Bolingbroke. Thus when the descendants of the Duke of Lancaster seized power from the holder of the throne there was certain to be a conflict with the descendants of the Duke of York who had, as it happened, married the female heir of the line immediately senior to the Duke of Lancaster. Henry of Bolingbroke and Lancaster retained the throne he had seized from Richard II, but had to suppress various revolts. His son, Henry V, as a popular and successful warrior, had no problems over his title to the crown but when he died at the age of thirty-three he left a son and heir less than a year old. This infant was destined to have the most disastrous reign in English history.

But the succession of a minor would not have mattered greatly, had he been reasonably capable later, for the Lancastrian line was now well established; unfortunately this infant, Henry VI, was intermittently mad and never very competent when sane. Furthermore he married a French wife of great courage, skill and determination who was subject to vindictive and rancorous hatreds.

The Wars of the Roses were not a civil war in the sense that the term is usually understood. There was no ideology involved; it was a power struggle between two groups of over-powerful families. It did not involve the majority of the country, and the contestants, very wisely, took care that it should not disrupt production and commerce. Thus the Battle of Northampton was fought outside that city, whose inhabitants remained undisturbed, though doubtless alarmed. Periodically, noblemen changed sides; in the later stages the war was fought in bitterness and revenge for real or supposed wrongs, and any trace of higher motives disappeared. There was a regional aspect to the war in that London, the Midlands and the south-east were Yorkist, and the west, north and Wales were Lancastrian. There were of course discrepancies in this regional pattern, and we find Lancastrian supporters in the south and Yorkist supporters in the north.

The early years of Henry VI were years of almost unbroken misfortune. The conquests of his father, Henry V, were gradually lost, and as disaster succeeded disaster overseas they were matched by mounting turbulence and disorder at home. Soldiers who had spent all their previous lives in France came home ready to sell themselves to the most affluent trouble-maker they could attach themselves to. A considerable part of the recent French disasters could be attributed to the stupidity of Somerset, Henry VI's chief minister. Somerset's deficiencies and high-handedness were obvious to everyone except Henry and it therefore seemed like divine intervention when Henry went mad, and the Duke of York, the next in line for the throne, was appointed Protector. York put Somerset in prison and replaced Henry's incompetent ministers by able and responsible men. Unfortunately this happy state of affairs did not continue long; for Henry VI's wife, Queen Margaret, produced a son after nine years of barren marriage, thereby ensuring the continuance of the Lancastrian line, and Henry VI recovered his wits sufficiently to mount the throne again. Henry's first act on re-assuming power was to release Somerset and reappoint him chief minister.

It was the last straw. York, normally a mild and patient man, was stirred to action. He called out his retainers and friends and marched towards London. Henry VI met him at St Albans. The ensuing battle was far different from the later embittered blood bath but it was vigorous enough, and in the course of it Somerset was killed. York asked for forgiveness from the King, who was his prisoner, but also resumed his own position of supreme authority (1455).

But blood had been shed and Margaret was not likely to rest till York's had joined it. The pity of it all was that Henry himself, though not an able king, had a character which could fairly be described as being saintly; York, although not of quite such high standards, certainly had no wish to do more than use his abilities in the best interests of the country. Many of the other personalities whose fortunes – and heads – rose and fell were less villainous than mistaken. It has been aptly said that an imagined wrong is much more deadly than a real one. The Wars of the Roses were overfull of both.

In 1465 Henry, by merely exercising his constitutional rights as the monarch, was able to dismiss York's supporters from office. Nobody, not even York himself, was unduly disturbed. The hated Somerset was dead, and nobody wished to see a fratricidal war. But, with turbulent and over-powerful families, some of whom were richer than the King himself, with suspicion and bitterness on all sides, and large numbers of trained but not well-disciplined soldiers everywhere, there was clearly more trouble looming. Where would the next clash come?

Margaret, believing that York and his supporter, the young Earl of Warwick, would effectively prevent her son's ever attaining the throne, spent the next two years swearing in adherents to her son's cause: she distributed silver swan badges as symbols of allegiance to him. Some of her supporters were even more active than she was. They provoked a riot in London when the Earl of Warwick, captain of the Calais garrison, was on a visit to Westminster. Warwick was lucky to escape with his life; it was now clear that if he set foot again in England he might be assassinated or put to death on a trumped-up charge. His father, the Earl of Salisbury, who had vast estates in Yorkshire, decided that matters had now gone far enough and that the Yorkists should reassume power. He began assembling his retainers in Middleham castle, ten miles south-west of York, possibly with the intention of marching on London. The Duke of York was at Ludlow Castle (or perhaps close by at Wigmore) from which area he was able to rally supporters from Wales. Margaret, not unmindful of the dangerous concentration of force which would occur if Salisbury joined York, now intensified her recruiting in Lancashire and Cheshire. The outcome of this was that the Lancastrians soon mustered a very considerable force which was put under the command of Lord Audley; it was said to number nearly 15,000.

At the beginning of September 1459 Salisbury made his move. His force numbered about 4000. This was clearly not enough to capture London even if Warwick came over from Calais with a substantial force to attack from the other side. Henry VI had moved to Worcester where he had a useful force though not an army, and Queen Margaret was at Eccleshall where she was able to continue recruiting yet keep a wary eye open for any Yorkist moves. The whole atmosphere was very brittle. War was inevitable but neither faction knew when or where to strike the first blow. A wrong move could easily lead to bloody and humiliating defeat.

Salisbury's move towards Ludlow caught the Lancastrians by surprise, but Margaret, who was a strategist of no mean order, rapidly grasped the fact that she could catch him in a trap. Margaret had reasoned that Salisbury's army was bound to march somewhere through the Stafford–Stoke line and assumed that Eccleshall, lying fourteen miles south of Stoke, would be as good a place as any to intercept it. However, Salisbury's intelligence services were clearly as good as Margaret's, so he took the road through Newcastle-under-Lyme and marched swiftly towards Market Drayton. This outflanked Margaret but would not put Salisbury out of reach of Henry VI's troops later if the latter moved quickly enough, which was unlikely. Salisbury went through Market Drayton and camped just south of the town on the hill which to this day is known as Salisbury Hill. So far so good, and everything going to a neat though delicate plan.

But now Salisbury was due for a shock. His scouts came up with the highly unwelcome news that a large force of Lancastrians, estimated at about 15,000 but probably exaggerated, was a few miles to the north-west, under the

command of Lord Audley. Their camp may be seen today on
the map, marked as Audley Brow. Salisbury, although he had
a good position and was protected by the River Tern, decided
that it was not in his best interests to give battle then and
there. In consequence, he struck camp while it was still dark
and moved north-east with the intention of slipping up to
Nantwich; from there he might still outflank the Lancastrians.
However, on this occasion Audley was not caught unawares,
and was soon on Salisbury's heels. Salisbury gave up the
attempt to reach Nantwich and instead withdrew in an easterly
direction. Audley, knowing that he had superior numbers, did
not hurry overmuch, and keeping Salisbury's rearguard in
sight made a leisurely pace which enabled the rest of his army
to catch up with the vanguard.

There was, however, nothing leisurely about Salisbury's
activities in the remainder of his army. Having reached what
seemed to him an almost ideal ambush position he proceeded
to exploit its possibilities to the full. Just south of the present
A.53 the land falls away sharply into the bed of the Hempnill
Brook, a fast-flowing stream which doubtless carried more
water in 1459 than today. The bed of the brook is about
twenty feet wide; the sides rise steeply and then slope more
gradually. On the north side there was plenty of cover and
Salisbury deployed his troops in concealed positions with a
centre line confronting the Lancastrian advance, and the
remainder equally divided between two diagonally-stationed
wing formations. Immediately ahead of the front line he
ordered a trench to be dug which was filled with sharpened
stakes. His archers were mainly on the wings but there was a
reserve force immediately behind the centre line. In case
Audley should try to outflank this position, which was
presumably at that time the most fordable part of the stream,
he had stacked up his baggage-carts on the exterior lines.
These, if nothing else, would give protection from the cross-
fire of those rightly-famed Cheshire bowmen.

Salisbury's tactics were ingenious and daring but, of course,
he had no option but to make a bold move if he were to
survive at all. His aim was to draw the maximum number of

Lancastrians into a position from which they could neither extricate themselves nor use their weapons to good advantage, and at the same time to encourage them to pursue their disastrous tactics until they were hopelessly defeated.

The first Lancastrian wave rushed down the slope, crossed the brook and mounted the other bank. By now all formation had been lost but, no matter, the Yorkists were retreating. Excitedly the Lancastrians waved on their followers who, seeing that success was imminent, also poured down the southern slopes into the river bed. As they did so the first line came up the bank and obligingly fell into the trench full of sharpened stakes. The knights were in the most trouble but the general confusion here looked no different from any other battle of the time, and the rest of the Lancastrians were only too glad to push on to join in and share the victory. Soon the whole river bed was full of Lancastrians trying to cross. At that point Salisbury threw in his reserve line and opened up with his wing archers.

The scene in that hollow must have been appalling. As the first wave of Lancastrians and some wounded decided they had had enough and began to retreat, they were carried forward by the centre of the Lancastrian army struggling up from the hollow. By now the Yorkist bowmen were pouring arrows on to the closely-packed men and horses, as they floundered on the river bed. This, as it became churned up and blocked with the bodies of fallen men and horses, became a trap from which there was little hope of escape. Some in desperation tried to move downstream but the Yorkists were mindful of that and had blocked the way. Others, realizing there was no retreat but no way forward either, tried to creep along the north side of the brook and reach safety that way. The Cheshire archers, from which so much had been expected, were forced down the slope into the confused and closely-packed ranks below. Their little silver swans made them perfect targets. Horses were useless, for the far bank was too steep for them to mount. Only when a macabre stepping-stone of fallen bodies had piled up was it possible to get a few horses over. By that time some of the bowmen were said to

have changed sides and were fighting their way out through
Audley's rearguard rather than face the death-pit in the valley
below. Others had no choice. The slope toward the brook is
steep and once the army was set in motion there was no way
of stopping the onrush except by falling. And falling meant
being trampled to death. The first clash had occurred at
1 p.m. and all through that bright September afternoon
desperate men were trying to fight their way out of the deathtrap; others no less determined were resolved they should not.
The hours went by, the brook filled up with corpses – it was
said to have run red with blood for three days afterwards –
and still the Lancastrians could neither mount the slope nor
redeploy on the far side where they were also exposed to
Yorkist arrows. Knight after knight tried to lead a breakthrough but was brought down well short of success. Among
them were Venables, Dutton, Troutbeck, Leigh, Done, Eger-
ton, and Molyneux. Some rallied around Audley when in a
last final effort he forced his way over the stream, up the
bank, and on to the northern slope. Here, half-way up the
ridge, where his monument stands today, he too fell. It was
the end of the Lancastrian effort, and pretty nearly the end
of the Yorkist effort too, for by now their arrows had gone
and their losses had been by no means light. Some Lancastrians were now able to move down the river bank towards
Market Drayton but it only delayed the inevitable, for they
were caught in the meadow where the Hempnill joins the
Tern, and were slaughtered where they stood. But, of course,
there were also a few Yorkists too who became overconfident
in the wake of the battle. They were killed or captured when
they pursued too recklessly and ran into larger forces of
Lancastrians.

It was without a shadow of a doubt a brilliant and unexpected Yorkist victory. The Lancastrian losses were given
as 2400, and their humiliation was greater. But it was not
decisive, as Salisbury knew. If Margaret, five miles away, and
Henry, ten miles away, brought up their combined army, his
own mauled forces would be quickly battered into defeat.
Clearly he could not stay at Blore Heath; he must press on

with all speed and join the Duke of York at Ludlow. But once he set out for Ludlow his army on the march would be an easier prey than if it stayed.

Once more he used deception. Realizing that Margaret would think he would rest and celebrate his victory he set off again as soon as darkness fell. His men did not grumble; they knew their lives depended on this stratagem. But he left his guns behind with an Austin friar to fire them during the night. ('Save only a Fryer Austyn schot gonnes alle that nyght in a parke that was at the back syde of the fylde.' [*Gregory – 15th century*].) Queen Margaret's army, approaching the wood and hearing the guns going all night long, considered that Salisbury was celebrating his victory with drunken revelry. But the next morning when they advanced for the kill they found the woods empty except for the friar. Asked with some irritation what he thought he was doing, he replied that the army had gone and left him behind and that he had stayed where he was firing the guns because he had been afraid to leave in the dark.

Salisbury reached Ludlow, but his brilliant victory was wasted in the fiasco of Ludford which took place less than a month later, on 12 October, just outside Ludlow. There, realizing they were once more heavily outnumbered – perhaps 6–1 – the Yorkist army left the field during the night, and the Lancastrians were the victors in a bloodless battle.

Ironically Salisbury was killed a year later, after the Battle of Wakefield. Wakefield, which took place on 30 December 1460, was another tactically brilliant battle, almost modern in its concept, but this time the losers were the Yorkists. Salisbury escaped from the field but was captured and, in the rancorous atmosphere then prevailing, was put to death. His head was displayed on the gates of York. Next to his was the Duke of York's head, crowned by Margaret with a paper crown. On the other side was the head of Rutland, York's second son; he was seventeen.

THE BATTLE OF
EDGCOTE

26 July 1469

The ten years between Blore Heath and Edgcote were filled with a succession of battles, each bloodier than the last. One of the most extraordinary features of this war was the way fortune ebbed and flowed. As we saw, the Yorkists won brilliantly at Blore Heath but gave up without a fight at Ludford. The following July, Warwick, now at the peak of his military and political ability, won a crushing victory at Northampton. The Duke of York then took control of London and it seemed obvious to everyone that the Yorkists were now in an unchallengeable position. However, it did not appear that way at all to Queen Margaret who was busy rallying a formidable army upon the Scottish border. York set off north to settle matters once and for all. He took young Rutland, his second son, to give the youngster some more battle experience. With him also was Salisbury, the victor of Blore Heath; he was sixty. In medieval warfare boys went on campaigns as soon as they were strong enough to hold a sword. When very young they were kept at a safe distance from the fighting, after having helped arm their knights; thus they could quickly flee from a lost battle or, if their side won, they could join in the pursuit of the fugitives and emulate the callous ferocity of their elders. Occasionally plans went wrong. Rutland, although neither novice nor child in medieval warfare, had not yet received the command to which his rank entitled him. However, he failed to get away quickly when the Yorkists were defeated at Wakefield and was mercilessly killed by a Lancastrian paying off a grudge. Nor was Salisbury's age any safeguard. He was beheaded the day after the battle.

Wakefield was a tremendous shock for the Yorkists. Tactically it was remarkably close to their own unexpected victory at Blore Heath the previous year, but at Wakefield it was the

Yorkists who fell into the trap. And now it seemed as if nothing could stop the Lancastrians. They pushed on to St Albans and this time decisively reversed the defeat they had sustained in the first battle of the war. Fittingly, Warwick, the architect of the earlier Yorkists' victory at St Albans, was now in command of the defeated army.

But there was a cloud on the Lancastrian horizon. It was Edward, Earl of March, eldest son of that Duke of York whose head was now stuck on a spike at the gates of York, wearing its paper crown. Edward, only nineteen, but over six feet tall and a leader of outstanding ability, had already shown the military genius which would bring him the crown within weeks. Just before the Yorkist defeat at St Albans, Edward had won a brilliant victory at Mortimer's Cross in Herefordshire. Now he was hot-foot for London, where there was plenty of Yorkist support.

Margaret wavered. After letting her seven-year-old son decide what form of execution her prisoners should suffer after the victory of St Albans, she fell back towards the north where she knew she was safe. If Edward wanted to fight her, let him find her there. There she would give him a suitable welcome.

The outcome was Towton in 1461, the greatest, bloodiest, and most bizarre battle every fought on English soil. At the end of it there was no one to prevent Edward, Earl of March, taking the crown as Edward IV.

There were of course other battles after Towton, devastating though that had been. Other Lancastrians fought back at Hedgeley Moor and Hexham, and held out for a while in a few castles. But these were not serious opposition. Queen Margaret and Henry VI were fugitives; and the country was solidly Yorkist.

It is all the more extraordinary to find that in 1469, after eight years of consolidating his power, the brilliant Edward IV should be captured after the Yorkist defeat at Edgcote. Edward, however, had two dangerous enemies – the Lancastrians and himself. The Lancastrians he could usually overcome, but his own personal weaknesses were another matter.

Although brave as a lion, a military genius, and as enduring as a marathon runner, Edward had two fatal deficiencies. When not in danger he became a self-indulgent idler, and when the fighting was over could never remember the reasons which had caused it.

After Towton he left the 'mopping up' operations to his cousin, Warwick. Warwick was a first-class soldier in spite of his defeat at the second St Albans; he was not, however, the equal of Edward IV. Politically, Warwick was far superior to his cousin and if Edward had treated him with reasonable common sense the two would never have clashed. But common sense seems to have been notably absent from Edward. When Warwick had not merely crushed the last of the Lancastrian resistance in the north but also made an agreement with the Scots that they would no longer support Queen Margaret, he felt, rightly, that he was a soldier and statesman whose advice should be respected.

Edward thought otherwise. He considered that Warwick needed cutting down to size. When Warwick suggested that Edward should take a French wife, the King announced that he had just married a Lancastrian widow secretly. When this shocked Warwick, Edward flaunted his defiance by giving his new wife's family and friends various important appointments. Warwick's annoyance and discomfiture merely amused him and he decided to increase it by humiliating him still further.

But Warwick 'the Kingmaker' was also a proud man. He knew, better than most, that the Yorkist cause might have failed at St Albans in 1455 if his enterprise had not won the day, and he was not likely to forget the fact. He had, of course, served the Yorkist cause with unswerving loyalty. He was older than the King, and more experienced in war. In some ways he was as powerful.

At this stage the position was complicated by events abroad. Warwick had felt that an alliance with France would remove support from Queen Margaret and strengthen Edward's position. Edward decided otherwise. To humiliate Warwick he made an alliance with the Duke of Burgundy – who hated the King of France – and married his sister to the Duke. Warwick was given the humiliating task of escorting her to this marriage. Edward had now pushed 'the Kingmaker' too far.

Lancastrian resistance, although suppressed, had not been extinguished completely. For one thing there was the gallant resistance of Harlech Castle, which was now in its seventh year of siege. It was not, admittedly, a very intensive siege for the castle had access to the sea, but it was a long, gruelling process none the less. One of the besieged was the future Henry VII and it has been suggested that his experiences during the siege of Harlech contributed to his subsequent grudging outlook. The annoyance which the continued Lancastrian resistance caused to Edward was noted with approval by the King of France, and he helped to keep it going with cash payments. In June 1468 he had attempted to launch a vigorous attack on the Yorkists from near Harlech and thus relieve the castle. However, the scheme went awry. He had financed and transported Jasper Tudor with an army to north Wales in French ships, but, after the initial success of plundering and burning Denbigh, Tudor's army was soundly defeated by Lord Herbert, the besieger of Harlech. Soon afterwards Harlech itself fell. These events convinced Warwick that if his humiliating position were to be relieved he must take the initiative himself.

Warwick's subsequent actions did him little credit, but it should be borne in mind that Edward's ingratitude had placed him in an intolerable position. He chose to ally himself with the Duke of Clarence, Edward's younger brother, 'the false, fleeting, perjured Clarence', who was subsequently murdered by being drowned in a butt of Malmsey in the Tower of London. Clarence was considered too unreliable to hold any position of state authority but was heir to the throne, as Edward at that time had no sons. (When he did they became the unfortunate Princes who were murdered in the Tower in the reign of Richard III.)

In the spring of 1469 there was a Lancastrian rising in the north. It was led by a mysterious figure known as 'Robin of Redesdale', a person who has never been properly identified and now, of course, never will be. Many believed that he was

Sir John Conyers, one of Warwick's relations, though his aims, which included a better standard of living for the poor, hardly seem to put him in that environment. The first phase of the rebellion was defeated but then a second stage began, commanded by one Robert Hillyard, called 'Robin of Holderness'. This was even less successful than the other, and was defeated at York, after which Robin of Holderness was executed. But Robin of Redesdale was now active in Lancashire, with a larger army than ever.

Warwick at this time was in Calais where, unknown to Edward, he had married his daughter to Clarence. This daughter, Isabella Neville, was immensely rich and the marriage therefore made Clarence potentially richer than the King.

Edward, as usual, was slow to take action. Throughout his career he had often been dilatory to the point of disaster, though once roused he proved unstoppable. On this occasion he delayed a little too long.

In June 1469 he decided to move north and deal with Robin of Redesdale. He probably knew that Warwick was backing the rising but gave no special attention to the fact. He made a leisurely progress through East Anglia, assembling an army as he went. At Nottingham he learnt that Robin of Redesdale's army was no rabble but a well-organized and disciplined force. He decided to wait for reinforcements from Wales, which would be available now Harlech had fallen. They were commanded by Lord Herbert, who had now been awarded the title of Earl of Pembroke. Edward then heard the unwelcome news that Warwick had come from Calais with a substantial force and was now moving north. Edward was now in a trap. He was about to be caught between Redesdale's army marching south and Warwick's army marching north. Owing to his own dilatoriness he had so far assembled only a small force, assuming that Pembroke would be able to deal with Redesdale, and he himself would then arrest Warwick, whose army would not be large. His assumptions were all incorrect. Redesdale had come down from Lancashire much more rapidly than had been anticipated. Edward did not know exactly where this northern rebel had got to, but he moved back south-east so as not to be caught by the closing of the trap. Edward was right in thinking that Pembroke's force was on its way from the west but he could not know that Pembroke and his co-commander the Earl of Devon had quarrelled over billeting arrangements – always a delicate matter when accommodation is limited. In some fury, Devon had taken his substantial army to Deddington, a few miles farther south on the road to Oxford. There was a substantial castle there with a huge bailey and it was a reasonable place for a camp. Apparently this army had most of the bowmen. Pembroke, with a smaller force but by no means a bad one, decided to block the routes from Daventry and Northampton to Banbury. This could be done by siting his camp midway between the two roads, and midway also between Wardington and Thorpe Mandeville. Redesdale was in fact farther west but the position was strategically sound – provided Redesdale's army was not too formidable. Four miles north-east of Banbury, in exactly the place Pembroke wanted it, was a flat piece of valley known as Danesmoor. It was sheltered and it had water; it was concealed by three low hills. With luck he could stay quietly there while the full weight of the attack went down the Banbury–Oxford road and fell on Devon. If Devon won he would be so mauled as to be glad of assistance; if he lost he would have done so much damage to Redesdale that the latter's battered army would be no problem.

It seems almost inconceivable that Pembroke posted no sentries on those hills, but military history abounds with examples of commanders thinking that the enemy were so far away that the most elementary drills were neglected. But perhaps he did post look-outs and they fell asleep, or were quietly killed. Whatever the reason, he woke up on 26 July to find the hills occupied by Redesdale's men.

Pembroke was in a difficult position. Common sense told him that his forces were too small and too short of archers to do anything but retreat and try to re-form in a better position. But first he had to extricate himself, secondly he had to hold his army together; if not winning, they were quite likely to desert, or even join his opponents. He decided that boldness was the best and only possibility. He attacked.

The first objective was the hill to the north (near Edgcote Lodge). Without adequate cover from archers this was an expensive way of fighting, but his determined Welshmen clawed their way up the hill and took it. Half-way up this hill, and over to the left, is a grove of trees. As readers will have noticed on other battlefields it was the custom to plant trees on grave pits as some sort of memorial, and it seems most probable that this is all that remains of the former grove. And doubtless there were other grave pits of which no surface trace remains.

So far so good for Pembroke, but the cost had been enormous. He turned now to the second hill. Fighting his way along the crest of the slope, and using a pole-axe with deadly effect, he led his men to their second victory. He now had easy access to the road by Thorpe Mandeville and he would have been wise to have settled for limited success and broken off the engagement. But with complete victory in his grasp such an action would have been unthinkable.

He pressed on to the third hill – the one by Culworth. At this point matters began to go seriously wrong. Now more than ever he needed numbers. Redesdale's army, while holding him on the crest, was now fanning out and around him on to both sides of the hill. Pembroke had no one to stop them and soon had the humiliation of seeing the territory he had so painfully captured once more in Redesdale's hands. To his credit he showed neither fear nor dismay but concentrated on Culworth in the knowledge that once the last central point was captured the other area could be retaken. And it would have been so but for an accident of war.

On to the scene came a mob of irregulars from Northampton, not trained soldiers at all but a motley collection of plunder-seekers who had been assembled by Sir John Clapham, a Lancastrian. As this force came into sight they shouted 'A Warwick, a Warwick' – a battle-cry which had been heard on many a field in the past fifteen years. Pembroke's men

promptly assumed that this was the vanguard of the Earl of
Warwick's army and that further resistance was hopeless. They
fled. As they broke in disorder, Devon who had now come
up from Deddington saw the scene, with Warwick's banner
of a bear and ragged staff waving over the hilltop. It was clear
to him that the battle was over and he did a very fast 'about
turn'. Victory was thus thrown away.

Losses had been high on both sides, and remarkably even;
2000 Welsh and 1500 English. The inevitable executions
followed. Many knights and esquires had died in the battle
or there would have been more scenes of vengeance afterwards.
Pembroke and his son were stoned and then executed; Devon
was beheaded in Somerset, and Rivers at Kenilworth.

Edward heard the news of Edgcote at Olney, Buckingham-
shire. He was not dismayed; he had fought back from worse
positions. But his confidence was not shared by his followers;
they deserted wholesale. Finally he was taken into custody
himself and kept under guard at Warwick Castle.

But Warwick was fighting a losing battle. He did not wish
– yet – to throw in his lot with the Lancastrians, and he dared
not aspire to the throne – although it could easily come to his
descendants. Having extracted a promise from Edward that
he would behave in a more responsible manner, he freed him.
Once more Edward became King in fact as well as name.

The sequel will surprise nobody. Once more Warwick and
Edward quarrelled. In March 1470 Edward raised an army to
defeat a rebellion in Lincolnshire. He did this with such swift
efficiency, at Empingham in Rutlandshire, that it became
known as Lose-coat field; it was said that the rebels threw
off their coats to run away the faster. Warwick and Clarence,
realizing that this was an event full of foreboding for them
too, wasted no time in leaving the country. They would return
– but each to his individual disasters.

THE BATTLE OF EDGEHILL

23 October 1642

Edgcote, which we described in the last chapter, was one of the last battles in the Wars of the Roses. Edgehill, which we examine next, was the first battle in the Civil War, and occurred nearly two hundred years later. During the interval the country had been mercifully free from civil war, although English soldiers – and sailors – had often been engaged in warfare overseas. There had, of course, been many military developments since Edgcote had been fought out with pole-axe, spear and bow. Of these more later.

The Civil War was entirely different from any earlier wars in England. All its predecessors had been inter-baronial struggles in which one large faction had fought with another. Although such conflicts as John against the barons in 1215, Simon de Montfort against Henry III in 1265, Edward II against the barons in 1322, and the Wars of the Roses during the mid-fifteenth century had all ostensibly been wars fought for the oppressed against the oppressor, they bore no relationship to democratic struggles as we understand them today. But during the reigns of the Tudors – Henry VII, Henry VIII, Edward VI, Mary, and Elizabeth I – the monarchy had become less absolute, power had shifted to the emergent middle classes, and the old aristocracy had declined in strength and influence. Admittedly most of the more turbulent and powerful families had been killed off before Henry VII came to the throne, but this did not mean that others could not have risen to take their place if there had been a power vacuum. By the time Elizabeth was on the throne the pattern of English politics had been established, although she herself was fighting a rear-guard action for the maintenance of royal power. However, Elizabeth was a realist and, being a woman as well, she was able to make the best of what seemed to her a not entirely satisfactory situation.

Her successor, James I, was aptly nicknamed 'the wisest fool in Christendom'. He had plenty of learning but no wisdom. He suffered from two delusions: one, that he was king by divine right, and two, that he could ignore the nation's laws and customs if it suited him. When he died in 1625 the country welcomed with relief his son, Charles I, who seemed in every way a much more attractive and balanced personality. Alas for hopes. Charles held many of his father's beliefs and had the courage and conviction to maintain them even in the face of the most obdurate resistance. There were, of course, plenty of faults on both sides. To Parliament, Charles appeared a dangerous fanatic who was trying to put back the governmental clock some two hundred years; to Charles, Parliament seemed to be full of misguided and obstinate men who would unheedingly destroy the kingdom, the Established Church, and the dignity of the throne. An added complication was that there were sharp divisions of opinion among the supporters of both sides. Charles undoubtedly acted very foolishly at times, but his mistakes were matched by those of his opponents. Unfortunately most people are brought up to see Charles as an obstinate tyrant whose people rebelled and, after a suicidal war, beheaded him. In fact some of Charles's actions, although arbitrary, ultimately benefited the nation: 'Ship Money' is an example. War became inevitable when Charles went to the House of Commons, with 300 men, to arrest his five chief opponents. They were in fact in touch with a Scottish army which had crossed the border, with the intention of coercing him into establishing a Presbyterian Church, so he had some justification in suspecting them of treason. However, the Five Members had received advance warning of his intention and disappeared. Charles then left London and never returned until he was brought back by his Parliamentarian opponents.

It was obvious from the beginning of 1642 that civil war was inevitable and both sides began making preparations for it.

Once war was certain, and during the course of it, the

dilemmas which had confronted Members of Parliament were presented to ordinary families. Just as today a family will often vote Conservative or Labour without having much sympathy for personalities or programmes but supports it as the better of two bad alternatives, so feelings were mixed in the Civil War. It was certainly not a class war, for plenty of the nobility fought against the King; conversely it had certain feudal aspects, for some of the landowners were able to take their tenantry to battle without any more opposition than barons had experienced in the Wars of the Roses. Allegiances were partly regional, for Parliament had the enormous asset of London, Bristol, Hull and Plymouth (the main ports), and many other large towns. However, Oxford, Newark, Worcester and Chester remained firmly Royalist.

With London went much of the south-east and Home Counties, though of course these areas also had pockets of Royalist sympathizers. Certain areas changed hands during the war. Bristol fell to the Royalists in 1643 but could never rival London as a strategic asset. Wales was almost completely Royalist, and remained so. The navy, with the exception of a few officers, was strongly Parliamentarian; this did not mean that Charles was entirely without shipping, for his supporters managed to produce a small navy by sheer ingenuity, but the defection of the navy was a great blow to the Cavalier cause. The war produced great flexibility in improvization. Oxford became a capital city with its own Parliament and administrative offices. Uniforms, swords, pikes, armour and gunpowder were manufactured, training was organized, resources were co-ordinated. As in other wars, even as late as the Second World War, people donated their personal possessions without demur. Superb family and college plate was melted down for the intrinsic value of the metal. This was bad enough, but it was matched by the destruction later of other beautiful objects – such as stained glass – by over-zealous Puritans who thought that plainness and ugliness denoted sincerity and progress.

Both armies were composed of cavalry in regiments of approximately 500; dragoons – who were mounted infantry –

armed with carbines and swords; infantry who carried pikes, muskets and swords; and artillery who had a variety of pieces ranging from 64-pounders to 5-pounders.

Numbers tended to fluctuate. An infantry regiment nominally had a strength of 1200 but was seldom up to this figure. The infantry, which consisted mainly of conscripts, was divided into pikemen, who were placed in the middle, and musketeers on the flanks. Most of their muskets were matchlocks with a range of 400 yards, but these could fire on average only once every three minutes. The front rank would fire, step to the rear, and the next rank took their places. This provided a steady fire provided the wind did not blow away the powder from the pan nor rain extinguish the match. Wheel-locks – with a flint and a process like a cigarette-lighter – were less vulnerable to weather but too easily damaged and thus made unworkable. However, musketry fire did substantial damage. When a musketeer had fired his twelve rounds – and sometimes before – he closed up to the pikemen where they both withstood the enemy charge, whether by cavalry or infantry. The pikeman had an eighteen-foot pike, and needed to be well disciplined and drilled if he was to do more damage to his opponents than to his own side. When pikemen met pikemen this became known as 'at the push of pike'.

Pike drill may be seen sometimes performed by units of 'The Sealed Knot', the society, some 3000 strong, which re-enacts battles of the Civil War in costume. It was founded by Brigadier Peter Young, who is a great authority on the Civil War – and on many other wars too – and now has branches all over England where its men and women (and even junior) members disport themselves at weekends. (The only qualification for entry is an interest in practical military history.)

The armies in the Civil War were tiny by modern standards, varying in size from 5000 to 12,000. In some ways this was an advantage, for communications were poor, maps were so inaccurate as to be almost a liability, and telescopes (known as 'perspective glasses') and watches were very rare indeed. The lack of watches made any concerted, timed attack impossible.

One feature of the Civil War which is often overlooked is its length. The first phase lasted from 1642 till 1646 – four long, bitter years. To many, it then seemed all over, but in fact five more years would pass before the last shots were fired. King Charles I was executed two years before the last phase of the war finally ended. In that war, as in many since, it was not the shock of battle or the list of casualties which produced the strain but the long, apparently unending struggle in which ordinary life was totally dislocated. At such times it seems as if the world will never be the same again. And, indeed, often it is not.

Although war was inevitable during 1642, neither side was ready to fight for most of that year. Charles raised the standard at Nottingham on 22 August but was not by any means ready at that date; he was short of both men and guns, and, if the Roundheads had tried to capture him, it is unlikely that his army could have stopped them. Parliament already had 15,000 men commanded by the Earl of Essex. Essex was an experienced soldier but was lethargic. He had no cause to love the Stuarts, for, some thirty years before, one of James I's favourites had seduced his wife, contrived a humiliating divorce, and then married her with James's approval. However, James's upstart favourite – who had now been made an earl – had not stopped at murder to help his plans along, and this fact now came out. Even James could not wink at this, and the two were put on trial and subsequently convicted. Essex was doubtless well rid of his former countess but the circumstances of the divorce soured him for life. The commander-in-chief of the Royalist army was Lord Lindsey, but the outstanding leader was Charles's nephew, Prince Rupert of the Palatinate, who was General of the Horse. Rupert was a brilliant all-round soldier (and subsequently a most capable Admiral). He was twenty-three at the start of the war but had already commanded a cavalry regiment at the age of sixteen, when he had been taken prisoner; he had spent the subsequent three years' internment studying his profession.

After raising the standard, Charles would have liked to have marched straight to London, but with Essex in his path, with twice his numbers, this was not practical. Instead, he moved towards Shrewsbury, planning to pick up reinforcements on the way. He arrived there on 20 September.

Essex moved towards the west also, but without any very clear idea of where he should be going. Somewhere, for all he knew, Charles might slip past him and head for London. As a middle course, he moved towards Worcester. After a brisk skirmish, his forces occupied the town. He then stayed there though he should have merely used it as a base while he headed off Charles from London. But while Essex was still pondering on the advantages which the possession of Worcester gave him, Charles slipped by him and reached Edgehill, four miles south-east of Warwick. When Essex realized what had happened he set off in pursuit and came to Kineton.

Now Charles was in a quandary. Should he press on and hope to capture London, with Essex crowding hard on his rear, or should he turn and give Essex a bloody nose? Encouraged by Rupert he decided on the latter course. Essex's lethargy once more betrayed him, for if he had pressed on while Charles was still collecting up his detachments he could have outmanœuvred the King and linked up with his own base in London. Instead he allowed Charles to make his dispositions along the Edgehill ridge.

Edgehill – which was once called Ratcliffe or Redcliff – is a three-mile sandstone ridge which rises sharply out of the plain – at times almost sheer but with some very steep paths; it faces north-west. It is now partly wooded but was then almost entirely open. There was some scrub on the fields at the base.

Both armies at this stage had a strength of 13,000 men, but the Roundheads were superior in infantry, the Royalists in cavalry. This being the first major battle of the war it had, inevitably, an indecisive beginning. Neither army wished to take the initiative and lay itself open to a brisk counter-attack. The Cavaliers might have remained on the ridge for days, blocking Essex's path to London, yet been unable to go ahead themselves, had the deadlock not been broken by a Roundhead gunner who sighted Charles and fired at him. Charles was on Knowle Hill. The shot fell short, landing on Bullet Hill, but it was enough to decide the King that it was time to teach the Roundheads their lesson. Abandoning his strong position he moved carefully down the steep slope and deployed on the plain below. At 1 p.m. the two armies faced each other midway between Kineton and Radway. Formation was as described above: infantry in the centre, cavalry and dragoons on the flank. But within that bare description of disposition there was much that could be said. Both armies were amateurs; neither had had anything but the most rudimentary training; and the Cavalier foot were deployed in the Swedish manner which none of them properly understood, and they were also very shallow. The Roundheads were a little deeper but still in two lines, each probably six deep. This would have given them a front of ten miles with the centre on the Kineton–Radway road. The right was probably resting on the Oaks plantation. The Cavaliers apparently made no attempt to outflank them although they scattered the dragoons on both of the Roundhead flanks.

The centre of the battle may be identified from the names on the map – Battle Farm, Grave-Ground, etc. After the initial tentative moves to close there began a not very effective artillery duel. Rupert, fretting to take the initiative, then charged straight at the Roundhead cavalry who were stationed on the left. The effect of the arrival of this brilliant and aggressive force was too much for the earnest but untrained Roundheads. Between King's Ley Barn and Kineton they broke ranks and tried to flee. Even the neighbouring infantry decided that the Royalist cavalry was too much for them. But it was also too much for Rupert's Cavaliers. They decided that the battle – and perhaps the war – was now won, and swept on towards Warwick. However, after two miles, they ran into some Roundhead reserves. They were commanded by a Captain Cromwell and, ominously, this hastily-assembled force checked the brilliant Cavalier attack.

Quite unknown to Rupert, an almost equally brilliant

Cavalier cavalry success was occurring simultaneously on the left flank; this was commanded by Lord Wilmot but, whereas Rupert had gone too far, Wilmot's action went too wide.

Equally unknown to both of them was that the infantry had met in the centre. The Cavaliers had apparently gained a psychological advantage by firing their muskets as they advanced, and in the opening stages pushed back the Round-head infantry. But their triumph was short-lived. Soon they settled down to some indecisive slogging 'at push of pike'. After an interval they broke off this close-quarter fighting and fired their muskets desultorily at each other.

But matters were not static elsewhere. Rupert's cavalry were somewhat disorganized, some having decided, now the war was apparently won, to plunder the Roundhead baggage in Kineton. After a two-mile charge they were of course so dispersed that Rupert could scarcely hope to re-form them. Wilmot's contingent, not having gone so far, were in slightly better case, and some of them turned and came back towards the centre.

At this point, Balfour, commanding the Roundhead cavalry, decided to take a turn in the game. Advancing from a point just behind Battle Farm, parallel with the Radway–Kineton road, he came forward in two separate charges, driving for the Royalist centre and left. The Royalist left consisted of untrained Welsh infantry who – good though they could be on other occasions – were right out of their element here. Accord-ing to Roundhead sources, they disappeared from the field forthwith. Balfour's cavalry was now up at the centre, right up by Battleton Holt. Here they captured Feilding, commander of the centre brigade, and some other senior officers. They were now also among the Royalist guns, which they wished to spike but could not through lack of nails. However they immobilized them so that the Royalists would not be able to salvage them; they also killed the gunners. Balfour then retired. The problem with cavalry successes was to consolidate them. Unless there was infantry in close support, cavalry gains could not be held. (This fact made the Charge of the Light Brigade in the Crimean War as wasteful as it was spectacular.)

However, frustrating though Balfour found it to have to retire, he did not waste time nor emotion but now applied himself to where he might be most effective. As the Round-head infantry advanced to the Royalist centre, Balfour wheeled his cavalry and came in on the Royalist flank. The shock sent the whole Royalist line reeling back. The Royalist standard was captured and the Royal standard-bearer, Sir Edmund Verney, killed. The Royalists fell back to a new line behind the brook.

And then, at this critical stage, the battle petered out. Fighting still went on, and men were killed, but drive and concerted purpose had left the field. Both sides were exhausted, and both undoubtedly confused. It is one thing to fight a battle, another to win it, and yet another to be able to profit by your victory. This is where the much-maligned staff is at its most useful. But neither side had a proper staff.

When Rupert at last appeared back on the field, dusk was falling. He has of course been much criticized for allowing his cavalry to ride right off the field in an impetuous charge, but restraining a successful cavalry charge requires superhuman powers. Prince Edward (later Edward I) was criticized for a similar action at the Battle of Lewes in 1264, when he returned to find his side had lost the battle. Rupert did not have the embarrassment of finding a lost cause but, even if he had, it would not have been possible for him to do anything about it. His men, and still more their horses, were completely blown, and to attempt to mount another attack was clearly impossible. Nor were the Roundheads in any better shape.

The verdict of history was that Edgehill was a drawn battle; but there are some who argue that, because Charles finished the battle nearer London than the Roundheads did, and was able to make Oxford his headquarters, then this must be accepted as a Royalist victory. Certainly Charles held the ridge while Essex retired to Warwick leaving many of his guns on the field. Essex may be said to have lost the battle but it is difficult to claim that the Royalists had had the better of the fighting.

Described like this it might appear that Edgehill was a

fairly gentle conflict. It was by no means so. Casualties were high on both sides. Cromwell was disgusted with the quality of some of the Roundheads whom he described as 'old decayed tapsters and serving-men', but they stood and fought, apart from the wings who were simply brushed away by the cavalry charges. There was heavy fighting around Battleton Holt, which did not exist in 1642 ('holt' means a wood) and trees may well have been planted to mark grave pits. Little Graveground contained 500 bodies; Great Graveground close on a thousand. There were other pits also, and there are parts of the field where the number of bullets and cannon-balls indicate the intensity of the fighting – and thus casualties. One of these areas is Lower Westcote Farm.

The visitor can look over the field from the top of Edge-hill, particularly from the Edgehill tower, and can also drive around it. To walk the centre of the battlefield requires permission from the commanding officer of the Ordnance Depot which occupies most of the site; it is not wise to venture on Ministry of Defence land in these security-conscious days without preliminary written clearance. But, as a view of the field and the whole feel of the battle can be obtained from the perimeter, many visitors will be content with that.

Charles stayed on the field the night after the battle, making himself as comfortable as possible in King's Ley Barn. He thought the Roundheads might renew the struggle as they had received substantial reinforcements by then but they did not and he moved on to Oxford. In spite of having lost his standard in the middle of the battle, he was fortunate in having it back, for it had been recaptured by one Captain Smith, who was knighted for his courage and enterprise.

But advantage – or victory – was frittered away. Charles's only hope of winning the war was to capture London at the earliest opportunity and hold it. Without it he was certain to be defeated, through lack of money and materials if nothing else. Instead, he lingered in Oxford. Essex was scarcely more enterprising but he did make an effort to outflank Charles by marching, though sluggishly, in a south-easterly movement.

On 4 November 1642 Charles reached Reading, being then slightly ahead of Essex who was still only at Woburn. Even then Charles did not press on, and it was nine days later before he confronted the City Trained Bands, 24,000 strong, at Turnham Green. Meanwhile Prince Rupert had won yet another of his swift victories at Brentford but there were another 3000 Roundheads guarding the Thames bridge at Kingston. The Royalists were in fact outnumbered by some 1000 men. Turnham was a critical point in the war, and it was a battle which was not a battle. Charles, seeing the strength of the opposition, paused and redeployed at Hounslow. Essex advanced and retook Brentford. The conflict was still wide open. A swift drive by Charles, headed perhaps by Rupert, might have punched a way through the enthusiastic but battle-inexperienced trained bands. But Charles hesitated. After a few days at Oatlands Palace, Weybridge, he retired to Reading. Both armies then went into winter quarters.

THE BATTLE OF
CHALGROVE FIELD

18 June 1643

Edgehill was not by any means the only scene of conflict in 1642. Battles, small or large, were taking place all over the country as Cavaliers and Roundheads struggled for control of their own districts. In the eastern part of the country it seemed as if the Roundheads were invincible, for they captured the whole coastline and hinterland from Hull to Portsmouth. In the west, it was a very different story, for Hopton decisively thrashed whatever opposition the Roundheads could mount in Cornwall and Devon. In Wales, everywhere but Pembroke fell to the Royalists. In the north, there was a bitter struggle between Lord Fairfax, an ardent Parliamentarian, and the Marquis of Newcastle, an equally convinced but more energetic Royalist. At the end of it Newcastle controlled the north from Newark to Scotland, with the important exception of Hull, which he could not take. By the end of 1642, both sides believed that they had only some unimportant clearing operations to finish in the areas they had overrun before engaging in a final decisive battle with the main opposition elsewhere. Both were of course completely wrong. But they went into winter quarters reasonably well satisfied with themselves. Winter campaigning was considered impossible for reasons explained earlier in this book, but that did not inhibit skirmishes and sieges.

During the winter there were renewed attempts at negotiations which proved quite fruitless because neither side would compromise. Yet both realized that the struggle was costly and suicidal. The strain of providing food, clothing, and especially pay was an almost insurmountable burden, particularly for the Royalists. Nor were all parts of the armies in complete sympathy with each other, and it was by no means unknown for one regiment to loose off a few shots in the direction of another of their own side. Other armies have occasionally smiled frostily when one of their more exuberantly conceited regiments is having a bad time from the enemy, but it is highly undesirable that they should assist the process in any way.

The year 1643 was destined to be a year of battles, but this was not particularly apparent at the outset. During the early months, Charles was trying to improve his position in the Midlands and Prince Rupert took Cirencester on 2 February. Essex remained dormant apart from authorizing an attack on Brill (north-east of Oxford), led by John Hampden, which was repulsed. Sir William Waller was more effective. He cut two Royalist regiments to pieces at Winchester, and followed it up by capturing Farnham Castle, Arundel Castle, and Chichester. He then set up his headquarters in Bristol and thus effectively barred the Royalists from contact with their supporters in the far west and South Wales.

Confined in the west and with Essex in force in the south-east, Charles drove hard at the northern Midlands. Royalists captured Ashby-de-la-Zouch, Tamworth, Stafford and Lichfield. The Roundheads countered this by sending Lord Brooke to rally the opposition. Lichfield came under siege twice, and there was hard fighting around Birmingham. Success in this area would effectively cut off the northern Parliamentary forces from the south, but equally Waller's masterly campaigning in the west meant that Charles in Oxford was cut off from his western supporters and threatened by Essex in the south. Nevertheless, Charles had evolved a strategy which might perhaps win him the war. It was to hold Essex's army while the Marquis of Newcastle brought down his great army from the north, and the Welsh and western armies forced a way past Waller. Then, with the whole Parliamentary army in confusion, Charles planned to push right through Essex's army and all three Royalist contingents would then link in the capture of London.

For a time it seemed as if this plan might succeed. April was not perhaps a very happy augury, for Essex moved up and besieged Reading on 16 April, and Charles, with Prince

Rupert and Prince Maurice, failed to relieve it; they were defeated at Caversham Bridge on 25 April, and Reading fell to the Roundheads on the 27th. Soon after this Essex's army was gravely weakened by disease. Slowly and indecisively he moved up towards Oxford but by mid-May the position was changing rapidly in the Royalists' favour. A huge convoy of arms and ammunition reached Oxford on 15 May and from then onwards the Royalists were the equals of the Roundheads in numbers of properly armed men. The day after the arrival of this vital convoy, the Royalists received equally welcome news from Stratton, in Cornwall, that Hopton had achieved a decisive victory over the Roundheads. This latter event meant that Waller was no longer able to bar Charles from his west country supporters though he could still do so from his Welsh ones.

On 10 June Essex was at Thame. He was still very hesitant but he had sent a detachment to occupy Islip as a preliminary to a further advance on Oxford. Perhaps he felt that to ask for more from his disease-battered army before he paid them would be asking too much. He knew that a convoy bringing £21,000 was on its way to him, and he felt that the arrival of this would put his men in a good mood for further activity. However, he was not the only one who knew about the convoy, for one of his mercenaries had deserted to the Royalists a few days before, and given the news about the convoy to very interested ears.

On 17 June Prince Rupert set out from Oxford with a force of just over 2000. It comprised three regiments of horse, one of dragoons, a mixed group of horse and dragoons numbering 150, and 500 foot.

The speed and unexpectedness of this move took the Roundhead outposts by surprise. Rupert overwhelmed Tetsworth, Postcombe and Chinnor in quick succession. Chinnor put up more of a fight than the others and there were a number of casualties but Rupert did not linger there; he set the town alight and rode on.

But the convoy which should be lumbering somewhere towards Thame, and should undoubtedly be in this region, was nowhere to be found. If news had got to the Royalists about the convoy, other news had also certainly got back to the Roundheads about Rupert's raiding party, and the convoy had briskly dispersed. Where it had concealed itself in that tangle of woods and thickets could not easily be discovered — certainly not by a small detachment venturing into enemy-held territory where the whole countryside would now be alerted. Furthermore Essex's army at Thame would wish for nothing more than to cut Rupert off before he could get back to Oxford. It would be madness to try to go back the way he had come, so he moved off in a southerly sweep, planning to cross the river at Chislehampton Bridge. What he did not know immediately was that John Hampden, one of the original 'Five Members' and a great fighter in every sense of the word, was at Watlington. When the news was brought to him he realized that although Hampden's force was small, perhaps not much over a few hundred, it could delay him long enough to allow other Roundhead reinforcements to catch up. Then indeed he might be in trouble, and, if he reached the bridge, be unable to cross it. His own men and horses were by now long past their best; they had been on the move for twenty-four hours. As they slowed down, Hampden's men began to be visible to the rear.

Rupert had to act quickly, which was no novelty to him. He sent a detachment of foot ahead to secure Chislehampton Bridge — for there was an excellent chance that the Round-heads would try to get there first. He then halted at Chalgrove Field, an open space one and a half miles east of Chisle-hampton. As usual he stationed the foot in the centre, placed the cavalry on the wings, and lined the hedges with dragoons. To his slightly irritated amusement the Roundheads adopted a similar formation, and advanced very slowly. On both sides the dragoons started picking off their opponents but the Roundheads made no attempt to bring the Royalists to battle. It was obvious that they wished to delay hostilities as long as possible and allow the reinforcements, which could not be far away, to catch up with them. And while they were in contact, the Royalists could not resume their journey.

Rupert, of course, would have none of this. He sat for a few moments watching these leisurely manœuvres, then behaved like a man annoyed by a few wasps. First he leapt straight into the Roundhead dragoons, who promptly fled, then he formed up his cavalry and gave the order to charge the Roundhead horse. Suddenly the entire picture changed; cavalry, foot and dragoons were all locked in desperate and bloody fight, pistols firing, swords flashing, men, horses, bodies, everywhere. In the middle of this essentially cavalry battle, John Hampden received two bullets in the shoulder. He knew that the wounds were serious and in great pain he rode back to Thame. Six days later he died, and even his opponents, who had little cause to love him, acknowledged that it was an appropriate end for a brave and resolute man. He did not see the end of the battle when a final Cavalier charge scattered the Roundheads in all directions. His plan had almost worked, for by that stage some of Essex's men had come up, but it had of course been frustrated by Rupert's initiative at the beginning. By the end of the battle the Royalists were nearly dropping with fatigue, but they had taken 100 prisoners and killed 45 of their opponents. As a mission the enterprise had failed in its main objective but had inflicted the greatest possible blow on enemy morale by killing Hampden.

The Hampden monument, on the corner, may or may not show the spot where he fell. Monuments are often - though not always - placed at spots convenient for them rather than on the exact place they are meant to mark. The battlefield is one of the easiest of all to visit, lying as it does just to the north of the junction of the B.480 and the Chalgrove–Warps-grove road. It was a cornfield in June 1643 and it was in 1972. It is impossible to predict what crop a farm will be growing next year, but there is a fair chance that the visitor will see the scene much as Rupert and Hampden saw it. Both were men of foresight. If perhaps someone had whispered to them as they confronted each other that one day an airfield from which men could fly in metal containers would skirt their battlefield they would have nodded and weighed the informa-tion without undue surprise or comment. Both were very open-minded men.

THE BATTLE OF
LANSDOWN

5 July 1643

The next significant battle in the eventful year of 1643 was in
the west country. Waller, some of whose successes were
mentioned in the previous chapter, now controlled Bristol and
Gloucester and had most of his army deployed in the vicinity
of Bath. He was a highly professional soldier and had learnt
his trade in southern Europe. Now, in his mid-forties, he was
one of the most respected of the Parliamentary generals.
Nevertheless, the Royalists decided that, reputation or not,
Waller could be and must be beaten.

To do so required a combined operation employing the
victors of Stratton, from Cornwall, and an army from Oxford
commanded by Prince Maurice. Hopton, the architect of the
Stratton victory, had no small difficulty in persuading his
officers to march their men from Devonshire when Plymouth
and Exeter, Bideford and Barnstaple, were all in Roundhead
hands and presumably ripe for the taking. The combined
army added up to 7000, of which just over half were infantry.
Waller was believed to have approximately equal numbers.

The delicate question as to which of these senior generals
should have supreme command was settled by Hopton being
given the main command, Maurice, however, being given a
free hand with the use of the cavalry. The Roundhead cavalry
was the equal of the Royalist and more numerous, but its
infantry was of lesser quality.

With Waller in such a strong position the Royalist strategy
was to split his armies and roll them up in two phases. This
would be easier to plan than to execute. During the month
of June they were tidying up the position in Somerset by
occupying such towns as Wells, Taunton and Bridgwater, and
at the end of the month they occupied Bradford-on-Avon,
Wiltshire, which is nine miles south-east of Bath. Bath was

the first objective, but to attack it from the south meant
negotiating the Avon under Roundhead fire and it was therefore considered more expedient to approach from the east.
To do so the Royalists moved in a north-westerly direction
but when they reached Monkton Farleigh and Waller had
given no sign of coming up on their flank they decided to
push on to a better attacking position north of the city. There
were indeed a few skirmishes in the area east of Bath, but
they were in the nature of light harassing brushes and not to
be taken seriously. A further five miles took the Royalists to
Marshfield where they camped on the night of 4 July. By this
time Waller was alert to the Royalist intentions. He realized
that if they marched south-east from Marshfield they would
soon occupy Lansdown Hill which was a valuable strategic
point; in order to prevent this, he marched out of Bath himself
and occupied the hill.

The armies were now five miles apart, and inevitably there
was some skirmishing in between. Very early on 5 July
Waller despatched a medium-sized force up to the Marshfield
outposts to upset the Royalists as they were making their
march dispositions. It created considerable alarm and disorder. However, Hopton soon had his men *en route* for Bath,
by the tracks which would take them past Lansdown. As they
approached the hill, they observed that the Roundheads were
so strongly entrenched, with earthworks and wooden defences
protecting their position, the whole area being screened by
flanking woods. Hopton and his officers decided this was
neither the place nor the time to attack. They halted and
skirmished but were not going to commit military suicide.
Pending a new strategy, the Royalists began to march back
to Marshfield.

It was an awkward moment, and the Roundheads of course
recognized it. The morale of a retreating army, even if it has
not been defeated, is not high, and it seemed very right to
Waller to lower it further by launching a heavy attack of
1000 cavalry and dragoons on to the retiring Royalists. And
at first it went remarkably well. The dragoons were able to
move up under cover of hedgerows and devastate the Royalist

flanks; the Roundhead cavalry charged into the Royalist rear and drove them so hard that they tangled with the unfortunate foot soldiers. It could not have gone better for the Roundheads. But Prince Maurice had introduced an interesting tactical disposition by stationing a section of foot among the cavalry. These were mainly the Cornishmen who had won the battle of Stratton and they began to give Waller's cavalry a lot of trouble. As this great harassing sweep – which included 1000 men – began to lose momentum and peter out, the Royalist cavalry put in two very sharp counter-attacks. Within the hour the Royalists had driven their opponents right back over Tog Hill to the base of Lansdown Hill, where they had stood despondently not so long before. It was 2 p.m.

Royalist morale was now at its peak, perhaps unduly so. Those strong positions of Lansdown Hill somehow seemed less formidable than before – at least to the Cornishmen who had already killed a substantial number of Roundheads. They also had tremendous faith in the leader, Sir Eric Hopton, who, ironically perhaps, was an old friend of Waller's from former campaigns when they had fought side by side. The fact that they were now opposing each other did not really disturb this long-standing friendship, but, of course, neither did their friendship diminish their military efforts.

The hill confronting the Cornish infantry is four miles long, and well wooded. The visitor will find the centre of the Roundhead position marked by an obelisk, commemorating Sir Bevill Grenvill (spelled Granville on the monument; contemporary accounts often show considerable variation in name-spelling), who was in command of the Cornish infantry, and was killed at that point. The battle which took place that afternoon was a tribute to the amazing fortitude and resolve of the Cornishmen. Whatever else happened, they ploughed on. Others supported them, fought alongside, and even forged ahead, but the steady rolling unrelaxed pressure which carried the day undoubtedly came from the tough and wiry Cornishmen.

They needed all the drive and resolve they could muster. As they came up through the woods, meeting frontal fire, cross-fire, and some heavy artillery which the Roundheads had placed on top of the hill, they paid dearly for their success. But they made their enemy pay too. Some regiments – which shall be nameless – found the pace and the fire too hot, and slipped away through the concealing woods. Some cavalry who were caught in plunging fire rode back to Oxford and gave an account of the battle which indicated how lucky and how wise they were to be there at all. They had of course been badly handled and misused but it was not an excuse the Cornishmen would have paid much heed to. For the cavalry – if they had been handled right and stuck it out – could have completed the victory when at last the foot and the musketeers reached the last barricade. For the sad part of it was that though they had reached the top of the hill there were still Roundheads in force behind a stone wall, and with guns too, and neither side had the strength for the last clinching effort.

Like Edgehill, the battle was ultimately indecisive, but like Edgehill it eventually became a Royalist victory. As darkness fell and neither side had the strength, ammunition, or even the will to renew the struggle, both commanders debated what to do. If the Roundheads attacked, the exhausted Royalists might be tumbled down the hill and utterly routed; equally, if the Royalists put in a final successful attack at dawn, the way to Bath would be open.

As it was, Waller, with the view of a campaigner rather than a battlefield commander, gave the order to return to Bath.

It should have been a moment of tremendous triumph for the Royalists. Although Grenvill had been killed, they had won the hill against impossible odds. And then, in the moment of elation, came an appalling setback. An ammunition cart suddenly blew up close to Hopton, wounded him, and blinded him. For a while he could neither speak, walk nor see. Apparently dying, he was carried off the battlefield past his dismayed army. First Grenvill, now Hopton. It would be limitless folly to try to press home the attack against Bath at this stage. Reluctantly, but not by any means slowly, the

Royalists abandoned their hard-won position and set off back in the direction of Oxford. But, of course, on Cold Ashton, Tog Hill, Freezing Hill and the slopes of Lansdown there were several thousand men who would never fight on that or any other field again.

THE BATTLE OF
ROUNDWAY DOWN

13 July 1643

As they moved back toward Oxford from Lansdown, the Royalists felt frustrated and dejected. Apart from the blow of losing such inspiring leaders as Grenvill and Hopton they had other troubles: they were short of ammunition, they were short of food, and the countryside seemed to be turning against them. They rested at Chippenham for two days and then moved on to Devizes; by this time Waller's cavalry were harassing the rearguard and the Royalists were glad to get into the town where they could collect their thoughts and decide on their next action. Waller had already invited them to fight it out by deploying his own army on Roundway Down, three miles north of Devizes, but they had not accepted the challenge. Hopton, who was now able to speak but not to walk, approved a plan by which his infantry and artillery would defend Devizes while the cavalry broke out and made for Oxford.

The Royalists were now in a sad case. They were short of ammunition, and one of the most vital deficiencies was match to take the light to the powder. Hopton ordered that all the bedcords in Devizes should be collected and boiled in resin; this ingenious expedient solved the match problem but there was still a grave shortage of powder and ball.

However, as Devizes held its hastily contrived outer defences, Prince Maurice succeeded in slipping round Waller and reaching Oxford – a night ride of forty-four miles. Time was no longer on Waller's side, as he doubtless realized, for the Royalists would soon be rushing reinforcements to help their comrades who were besieged in Devizes. Waller's forces, however, still outnumbered the Royalists, and as he redoubled his efforts to capture Devizes he also sent in surrender terms. Hopton appeared to be considering them but in fact was waiting for the relief he felt could not be far away.

The relief force was at Marlborough, fourteen miles off. It was commanded by Wilmot, whom we last spoke of at Edgehill. It was a wholly cavalry force but it had two light guns; its total numbers did not exceed 1800. On the morning of 13 July it was approaching Devizes which had been under heavy artillery fire for the previous twenty-four hours.

Waller, however, still had the initiative. He could turn on Wilmot's cavalry and deal with them in pitched battle, in which he outnumbered them, or he could draw them off with a portion of his army while he used the remainder to complete the capture of Devizes. He must not, of course, allow himself to be trapped between Wilmot's 1800 horse and Hopton's 3000 infantry from Devizes, even though he still outnumbered the combined Royalist force by over a thousand. What he could not have expected was that the Devizes army would stand idly by, in spite of Hopton's urgings, and let him annihilate Wilmot's relief force. Wilmot, unaware of the fate in store for him, continued along the old road from Marlborough to Devizes, which runs north of the present road and is in fact the track which skirts just south of Heddington. This road was (and is) crossed by another which runs south-west to Devizes, and the crossroads are right in the middle of Roundway Down where Waller had tried to tempt the entire Royalist army to battle just before they entered Devizes. It was, of course, a perfect place for a cavalry battle. To the north were Morgan's Hill and King's Play Hill, and to the south was Roundway Hill, then known as Bagdon Hill.

As Wilmot crossed the Wansdyke (a few miles from where the decisive battle of Ellandun had been fought eight hundred years earlier), Waller's army came into view over Roundway Hill. Wilmot had no doubt that Hopton's army from Devizes would be coming up fast to catch Waller in the rearguard and calmly made his battle dispositions. He might have been less sanguine if he had known the true state of affairs. Facing his left flank he could see a very formidable force, Sir Arthur Hazelrigg's 'lobsters'. They were, in fact, cuirassiers with close-fitting armour which was very difficult to penetrate.

Wilmot, being a cavalryman, turned his attention to the wings and hit both simultaneously with vigorous charges. This left the Roundhead infantry in the middle standing by inactive and unharmed apart from the occasional stray musket-ball which found a target in their ranks. They could not take part in the battle themselves for the wings were an indistinguishable fighting mêlée.

The scene at this point is best described in the words of Richard Atkyns, a cavalier who took part in the battle.

Twas my fortune in a direct line to charge their general of horse [Sir Arthur Hazelrigg]; he discharged his carbine first, and afterwards one of his pistols, before I came up to him; and missed with both; I then immediately struck into him and touched him before I discharged mine, and I am sure I hit him for he staggered and presently wheeled off from his party. Follow him I did and discharged the other pistol at him; and I'm sure I hit his head for I touched it before I gave fire and it amazed him at that present but he was too well armed all over for a pistol bullet to do him any hurt, having a coat of mail over his arms and a headpiece musket proof.

Atkyns was not to be put off:

I came up to him again and having a very swift horse stuck by him for a good while and tried him from the head to the saddle and could not penetrate him or do him any hurt; but in this attempt he cut my horse's nose that you might put your finger in the wound and gave me such a blow on the inside of my arms amongst the veins that I could hardly hold my sword; he went on as before.

And so the running fight continued. Eventually Atkyns was shot in the shoulder but not seriously.

There must have been a hundred or so fights like it. In the course of the battle, Waller's cavalry had been swung around so that the only way they could escape was to the west.

As they spurred their horses off the battlefield, hoping to find a point to regroup, they suddenly realized that the gentle plain over which they were galloping was a mere plateau. They were now at its edge – a drop of 300 feet. There was no stopping. Down that deathtrap hill they rode, slithered and fell, and many of their pursuers with them. This indeed was a bloody ditch. Not since Ashdown had there been a scene like it, and even then it was less dramatic. The unbelievable had happened. Waller's invincible cavalry had been put to flight by a force of half their number, and at the end of it had not merely been beaten but had been literally smashed to pieces. Even the Roundhead infantry, standing neglected in the middle of the field, had no conception of the disaster which had overtaken their army.

But their turn too was coming. Hopton's army, waiting in Devizes, had not taken long to make up their minds – particularly with him urging them on. Out they came, hoping to save Wilmot's cavalry from too severe a defeat, or perhaps to change probable defeat into narrow victory. As they breasted the hill all they could see was the Roundhead infantry, still uncommitted. On the flanks Wilmot's cavalry were regrouped to deal with this last target. The isolated Roundheads had no hope at all. On the one side, they took the shock of the Cornish infantry; on the other, Wilmot's triumphant cavalry. Six hundred were killed, the rest captured. It was a fitting end to a most extraordinary day. Never before had the Royalists had such a victory, and never would they do so again.

THE FIRST BATTLE OF NEWBURY

20 September 1643

The unexpected but extremely important victory at Round-way Down swung the war once again in the Royalists' favour. Prince Rupert lost no time in consolidating these gains. With a balanced force of cavalry, dragoons, infantry and artillery he moved promptly to Bristol and laid siege to the town. The ensuing battle lasted a day only but included more vigorous and continuous fighting than many a campaign on other occasions. Rupert himself turned the scales in one quarter, for he collected up retreating men and led them back into the fight although his horse was shot under him in the process. This siege, incidentally, was the last occasion when bows and arrows were employed by English armies. They were used by the Cavaliers in conjunction with fire-pikes to set the defences on fire. Stones were thrown and boulders rolled and in many ways this battle of Bristol bore close resemblance to the great medieval sieges.

Dorset and Devonshire soon fell to the Royalists although a few points still managed to hold out. Charles now decided to open up the road to South Wales, and promptly called on Gloucester to surrender. He was firmly but courteously refused. Prince Rupert would have liked to attack Gloucester forthwith and batter his way in, but Charles thought that the cost in casualties at Bristol had been so high that a second assault of that nature was not justified, however valuable the prize. Charles's action in deciding on a set-piece siege at Gloucester has been heavily criticized but there is as much to be said for it as against it. Elsewhere the war seemed to be going so well in the King's favour that his supporters might well have assumed that he would be back in London by Christmas. In the north, in June, Newcastle had beaten the Fairfaxes at Adwalton Moor, and at one moment it seemed

as if a Royalist rising in Kent might march on London and
seize power.

In this hour of need Parliament rose to the occasion with
remarkable vigour. Six regiments of London Trained Bands
were added to Essex's army, and supplies were found for the
entire force on an adequate scale. This gave Essex a total
army of 15,000, with which he marched to the relief of
Gloucester. Rupert had insufficient men to stop this huge
force and so had to keep out of its way as it pressed on
westwards; it relieved Gloucester on 8 September, arriving in
the nick of time, for Massey, the Governor, was down to his
last three barrels of powder.

However, Essex's move had put his army in a vulnerable
position. He was now between a hostile Wales, a hostile
west country, and Charles's Oxford army. Charles, in fact,
had moved quietly to Sudeley Castle, Gloucestershire, on
7 September. There he watched to see what Essex would do
to extricate himself from the middle of a triangle with three
hostile sides.

Essex moved up the Severn to Tewkesbury, trying to give
the impression he was going to attack Worcester instead of
slipping back to London. Charles promptly moved up to
Pershore so as to stay between Essex's army and the capital.
Essex then doubled back on the Cirencester–Swindon line,
reaching the latter on 17 September. Charles came back too,
marching parallel to but fifteen to twenty miles north of
Essex's army. Everything depended on who could reach Newbury first; if it were Essex, he would be within reach of
safety; if it were Charles, he could cut off Essex and probably
destroy his army, which by this time must be low on supplies,
and perhaps on morale too as any army must be if hunted
on a series of forced marches. Essex looked well set to reach
Newbury first, but Rupert put in a superbly-timed attack at
Aldbourne Chase, causing considerable confusion though little
real harm, and delayed the Roundheads so much that they had
to camp at Hungerford. Fortunately for them, the Royalists
made hard weather of this stage too and spent the night at
Wantage. When on the 19th the Royalists reached Newbury,

they found the Roundhead advance party allotting billets for the expected units of their own army. Essex by that time had reached Enborne, two miles west.

The First Battle of Newbury, which occurred the next day, was fought south of the town on the fields sloping down to the River Kennet. The Second Battle of Newbury, which we describe later, was fought north of the town, close to the River Lambourn.

The battlefield of First Newbury is now, inevitably perhaps, encroached on by new building. Fortunately some of the key positions are commemorated in the names of the streets. The area was, however, well enclosed in 1643, though by hedges not houses.

Morale in the two armies was in sharp contrast. The Royalists were in comfortable billets, had the satisfaction of knowing they had cut off their opponents from their base, and could surmise that the Roundheads were weary, short of food and supplies, and inexperienced in battle. This Royalist army had a good opinion of itself and its social importance, and doubtless looked forward to the thought of riding over and cutting up a few upstart churls the next day in the course of a brilliant victory.

The Roundheads were indeed in a poor way. They had marched for miles but apparently to no avail (if one excepted the relief of Gloucester). They had also lain up overnight in the wet and cold; however – as we saw at Towton (*Fontana British Battlefields: the North*) in 1461 – men can be nearly frozen to death overnight but fight like demons the next day if they are sustained by bitter-enough hatred. It was so at Newbury.

The only course open to the Roundheads was to force a way through on the meadows by the Kennet. It would not be easy because the Royalist cavalry would be expecting just such a move. Fortunately for the Roundheads, it seemed to be the only tactics the Royalists envisaged, for they had made no attempt to occupy Wash Common Farm or the patch of higher ground slightly north of it. This area is directly west of the Falkland Monument which is easily found on the A.343

just south of Newbury. The high points could have been
secured effortlessly without weakening the disposition nearer
Newbury, for the front there was narrow anyway. The armies
were equally matched in numbers, having about 12,000 each,
but the Roundheads had nothing to match the quality of the
Royalist cavalry.

The battle began soon after first light. The Roundheads
probed their way along the meadows and appeared to be
offering themselves as lambs for slaughter by the Royalist
cavalry. But, just as the battle settled to a grinding slog,
Royalist morale took a decided toss. Guns opened up from
the Roundhead right flank, from that very point on the 400-
foot contour line which the Royalists had failed to occupy the
night before. It was humiliating, and irritating, but not
disastrous. There were in fact only two light guns involved,
which the Roundheads had pulled into position during the
night, but two guns can do a lot of damage and the Roundheads, having got them there with difficulty, would not have
neglected to organize their defence.

Sir John Byron was now given the task of ejecting the
Roundheads and their two guns from this eminence, which
is known as Round Hill. It was captured, but the cost was
very high. Among the many who fell at that point was Lord
Falkland. Taking the Round Hill was a formidable achievement, for the Roundheads had a brigade on it by the time
the heavy fighting began; but taken it was.

Elsewhere, Prince Rupert's cavalry had charged the Roundhead infantry vigorously but without much effect. In the
meadows it looked as if a stalemate was developing. Artillery
on both sides was pounding away steadily. Both armies were
determined to cling to the part of the ridge they held and if
possible to extend their position, but each side was equally
determined the other should not. There was heavy fighting
along Skinner's Green Lane. Eventually it seemed to the
Royalists that their best chance was to knock a hole in the
Roundhead infantry, much of which consisted of inexperienced
Trained Bands. To their astonishment and annoyance, these
city regiments stood up to repeated charges and some remark-

ably accurate artillery fire. It was said that they far surpassed the Royalist infantry. Their desperate dogged resistance was a foretaste of the qualities of the great British regiments which would fight on less unhappy occasions than a murderous Civil War. Civil wars, when people of common heritage, kinship and interests fight each other, have rightly been described as 'unholy wars', but a redeeming feature of this one was that both sides showed the same tenacity and enthusiasm.

By nightfall both sides were thoroughly exhausted, but the Royalists had the more serious problems. The cavalry on which they depended so much had taken heavy casualties, and powder was so short that they were unable to keep up artillery counter-fire; in fact the Roundheads were firing three shots to the Royalists' one.

An urgent Council of War took place in Newbury that evening. Should Charles wait for the ammunition which was hourly expected, or should he withdraw to Oxford? If the ammunition did not arrive, he might be in a parlous state the next day, with his cavalry badly mauled, and nothing to fire from his twenty guns. Prince Rupert would have preferred to have stayed, but it was a bluff which might have been called. Essex might have renewed the fight the following morning, and, with conditions as they were, could have inflicted a severe defeat on the Royalists. Equally he might have decided it was impossible to break through, and set off back for Gloucester. But when he sent out patrols on the morning of the 21st he found that the Royalists had gone. His weary but elated army plodded on towards Reading. They were harassed by a few cavalry charges from Rupert on the way but there was no more real fighting. The First Battle of Newbury had been drawn, but there was no doubt in anyone's mind that it was a strategic victory for the Roundheads. Gloucester was still in their hands. The Royalist road to Wales was blocked, and Essex's new army had proved that it could stand up to the worst the Royalist cavalry could do to it. Altogether, at the end of a triumphant summer, matters began to look ominous for the Royalists.

THE BATTLE OF
CROPREDY BRIDGE

29 June 1644

Even though Newbury had been a strategic reverse, the
Royalists were still in a very strong position in the autumn of
1643. After their successes in the north and west it seemed
obvious common sense that Charles should not attempt what
he had thought about earlier in the year – a triple drive on
London. But, unfortunately for his cause, neither his northern
nor his western supporters wished to move far from their home
areas. Then followed the disaster of Winceby in October and
it suddenly became clear that the Roundheads had good
cavalry as well as good foot.

Even so, the future did not look too good to the Roundheads either. All their three main armies had taken hard
knocks and there was the problem of keeping pay going and
preventing desertion. Pym died in December, and he was a
more serious loss even than Hampden had been. Strenuous
attempts had been made to raise an army from Scotland, but
the price demanded by the Covenanters was thought to be
almost too high. There would be morning and evening
prayers, two sermons on Sundays, fearful penalties for loose
women and loose-livers who consorted with them; drunken-
ness and irreverent speech were virtually capital offences.
But 21,000 men are 21,000 men, and Parliament was prepared
to pay almost any price in this hour of need. Up on the
Border there were people who were a little sceptical about
how disciplined this host might prove to be, but for the most
part they were wrong. Charles meanwhile had arranged for
help from Ireland; the fact that his new allies were as
fanatically Roman Catholic as the Scots were Low Church
spread a feeling of gloom on both sides during the winter
of 1643.

With the spring the war quickly warmed up again. Waller

won a dramatic and unexpected victory at Cheriton (Hampshire) on 29 March 1644, and the Roundheads were equally active in the north. On 20 April York was besieged. Strategically this was very dangerous, for any attempts to relieve it would make the Royalist lines extremely vulnerable and perhaps lead to even more serious setbacks elsewhere. The Irish army, from which much had been expected, had been caught unawares and routed at Nantwich in January. Everything depended on what Rupert could do with a hastily assembled army from the north-west.

At that moment Charles turned to close friends and received extremely bad counsel. It was suggested that if he withdrew from Reading and Abingdon his army would be more compact and mobile. The first result was that Essex and Waller promptly reoccupied the two towns, thereby boxing him in more closely. Oxford, at any moment, might come under siege, and Charles's army become useless in the war. Hastily but without clear plans he moved out to Worcester. Massey was coming in from Tewkesbury; Charles's only hope was to make a swift drive and link up with Rupert in the north-west.

Astonishingly, Essex, renowned for his lethargy, now showed speed and resolution, but in the wrong direction. Without caring for protests, he set off to recover the west country. This took the immediate pressure off the King who now fell back to Woodstock. At that point his position changed dramatically. He regrouped his army, fitting it out with reinforcements from Oxford, and appeared about to launch an army of 10,000 into the thinly defended eastern counties. For a few days he had total victory within his grasp. He could have swung east and south and gone on to a virtually defenceless capital. But, instead, he hesitated.

Of all the unexpected twists in this remarkable war this was probably the strangest. At the beginning of June Charles had been in a trap. Then, owing to an inexplicable decision by Essex, the trap had been opened and Essex had departed to the west. That still left Waller with a large army at Kineton, but a few rapid moves could dispose of that danger.

But, instead of moving east, Charles marched his army

toward Banbury. On 28 June his scouts sighted Waller's army near Hanwell Castle, some 2½ miles north-west of Banbury. The Royalists therefore took up position at Grimsbury and both sides looked at each other's strong hill positions and pondered how to tempt the other into a more vulnerable area. There was considerable skirmishing between the cavalry of both armies, but it was obvious to Charles that this could go on indefinitely without drawing such a seasoned old warrior as Waller.

Charles then decided to move off. (Readers will note that the armies were now within a few miles of the site of the Battle of Edgcote (1469).) Charles set off in the direction of Daventry – the B.4036; Waller took note of what was happening and began marching in parallel, a mile away, up the A.423. This was not a very happy position for the Royalists, whose manoeuvres were in full view. Marching with another army on one's flank is a somewhat unnerving procedure; it is vastly better to be followed by an enemy, for then you can provide all sorts of little surprises for him in the form of ambushes or deceptive moves.

At this point news came in that there were Roundheads on the road ahead. Undoubtedly these would be planning to join Waller, so Charles sent his advance guard ahead to cut them up before they could do so. It obeyed its instructions so quickly that in no time there was a gap in the middle of Charles's column. Waller was not the man to miss such an opportunity and slammed in a two-pronged attack. The rear party was fortunate in finding a ford over the Cherwell at this point at Slat Mill and came right in behind Charles's rearguard. The forward prong bore straight on to Cropredy Bridge which it captured without trouble. Roundheads then poured across and drove hard towards Hays Bridge, passing on the way the tree under which Charles had been taking an early dinner only half an hour before. ('Lunch' was just coming into use to describe what nowadays might be known as a 'snack'. 'Dinner' denoted the main meal of the day, usually taken around 11.30 a.m.)

It could have been an instant Roundhead victory, but the

Cavaliers saw it otherwise. The Earl of Northampton, still in his teens but a veteran in war, put in a series of vigorous counter-attacks and hurled the Roundheads back over Slat Mill ford. Cleveland showed similar initiative, and battered the Roundheads who were now heading towards Hays Bridge. He held them at the point which might be described as Charles's dinner-table and then, aided by some useful attacks from Stuart Lifeguards, drove them right back across the bridge. In the process, the Roundheads lost all the guns they had just taken over the Cherwell.

But the river still separated the two armies, hot though the fighting was at the bridge and the ford. Eventually, after taking some heavy losses, the Royalists gained command of Slat Mill ford, but they could not force their way over the bridge. For a long hot summer afternoon Cropredy Bridge was the scene of brave and bitter fighting. As evening approached, Waller's army came under Royalist cannon-fire; it was said that target-spotting was done by the King through his 'perspective glasses' and that he also fired some of the cannon himself. By now Waller was withdrawing. Unfortunately for the Royalists they could not follow up their brilliant victory for the Roundheads were just about to be reinforced with another 4000 men. Nevertheless, Charles's Oxford army was safe from threat, Waller's army mutinied soon afterwards, and the King felt free to drive down to the west country and complete his unfinished business with the Earl of Essex.

THE SECOND BATTLE OF
NEWBURY

27 October 1644

While the Royalists were feeling reasonably pleased with themselves over the Battle of Cropredy Bridge, another and much greater conflict was looming. This was the huge, confused, but decisive Battle of Marston Moor, of 2 July 1644. Its result was that the Royalists were destroyed in the north, and one of its most disastrous effects was that the Marquis of Newcastle became so angry with Rupert that he refused to continue fighting for the Royalist cause.

But matters looked better in the south and west. After Cropredy, Charles had moved to Weymouth, then Tavistock, then Exeter. At this stage Essex was about to invade Cornwall, where he hoped to prohibit the export of tin on which Charles depended to pay for munitions.

As soon as Essex reached Launceston he realized the appalling mistake he had made. Charles was close by with a larger army. The outcome was the dramatic Royalist victory at Lostwithiel on 2 September 1644. Although this was a triumph for the Royalists in every way it did not take them much further towards winning the war. And it did little to offset the tremendous losses entailed by Marston Moor. And, dotted here and there over southern and western England, there were still formidable points of Roundhead resistance, as for example at Plymouth, Weymouth and Poole. Some Royalist strongholds like Banbury Castle (now completely destroyed), Basing House, and Donnington Castle (Newbury) were still under siege, and it did not occur to Charles to leave these places to their own devices while he made a decisive move to end the war by advancing to London. While he pondered on what to do next, vital time slipped away, and the Roundheads recovered from their reverses and rebuilt their armies. When, six weeks later, Charles came back to

Salisbury he could muster only 10,000 men, whereas his opponents had close on 17,000.

Nevertheless, the Roundheads retired gently in the face of the Royalist advance. On 18 October the Roundheads who had been besieging Donnington Castle fell back to Basingstoke. This meant that much of the Parliamentary army was now in north Hampshire but, in spite of his numerical disadvantage, Charles seemed intent on relieving Basing House. By 21 October he was at Kingsclere, ten miles away.

At this point Charles was prevailed upon to take advice. It would, of course, have been tantamount to suicide to press on to Basing, and instead he moved to Newbury, which was eight miles north-west. He then despatched a brigade to relieve Northampton Castle and waited to see what his opponents would now do. With luck they might draw away from Basing and give him a chance to relieve it. They did, but only to come to Newbury where Charles, having hived off the brigade, was now only 9000 strong. Against this the Roundheads brought 17,000 men.

This battle could have seen the end of the war. At the outset it seemed as if there was no hope at all for the Royalists. But Charles, who had a fine eye for a tactical site, had chosen wisely. The centre of his position was Shaw House, a formidable structure surrounded by earthworks constructed for some ancient but unknown battle. His right was covered by the Kennet and Newbury itself, his left by the Lambourn, and behind was the formidable Donnington Castle, with its massive drum towers, giving him perfect observation of his enemies. The position was undoubtedly a good one but not perhaps as good as it seemed to the Roundheads. To them it looked almost impregnable. In consequence they decided a single attack was impossible and resolved instead on the somewhat complicated device of an attack from front and rear simultaneously.

The rear attacking party was then allotted the somewhat exhausting task of marching an extra fifteen miles so as to approach undetected from the Wickham Heath direction. Much of the value of this move was lost by Charles's learning what was happening, and he made disposition accordingly. Had he known more about the numbers he might have attacked the frontal party which in fact numbered less than 5000.

The Roundhead attack was co-ordinated by cannon-fire. The Earl of Manchester was to attack from the east, while Skippon, Waller and Cromwell came in from the west. The plan miscarried. Whether Manchester did not hear the appropriate signal or merely thought it was Royalist gunfire is not known. However, when Skippon attacked west of Speen there was no response from Manchester. Nevertheless, the Roundheads were doing well enough. They rolled back the Royalists, some of whom began to flee in spite of Charles's efforts to check them. The situation was looking grim for the Royalists until Cleveland and Cansfield put in three tremendous charges which pushed the Roundheads right back to Speen. By now dusk was gathering, but at long last Manchester put in his attack. He was met by Lisle and temporarily pushed back, but numbers soon began to tell. After an hour's dogged fighting it was so dark on the battle-field that both sides hesitated to continue lest they should attack their own men. The Roundheads, having failed to co-ordinate in daylight, were apprehensive about what might happen if they continued their efforts in the dark. The gunners, not knowing what targets to choose, stopped firing, and the foot and cavalry disengaged.

Second Newbury had been as indecisive as First Newbury and once more Charles slipped away under cover of darkness. He rode to Bath where he joined Prince Rupert. His army withdrew north and were in Oxford by nightfall of the 28th. The Roundheads had had the best of the fighting but nobody enjoyed the fruits of victory. Even Donnington Castle was in Royalist hands and still holding out.

THE BATTLE OF
NASEBY

14 June 1645

The year 1644 came to an end with no sign of a breakthrough in the war for either side. Charles seemed the more active, and probably felt, with some justice, that if he had taken complete command from the beginning he might have won the war. His attitude in the continued negotiations with Parliament was noticeably harder.

At this stage Parliament took the steps which ultimately decided the result of the war. By the 'Self-Denying Ordinance' senior and less experienced officers were encouraged to retire voluntarily. That took Essex, Manchester, Waller and other commanders of unhappy record out of the firing-line altogether. Cromwell stayed, but, as he was the foremost cavalry commander of the day, that was no handicap.

Simultaneously the Roundheads overhauled the rank and file of the army. The 'New Model' was formed consisting of eleven regiments of horse – a total of 6600 – 1000 dragoons, and twelve foot regiments each numbering 1200. These were a combination of the best of the old armies plus a good number of pressed men. They were well armed, well clothed, well trained and well disciplined. They were also properly paid. Sir Thomas Fairfax was commander-in-chief with Cromwell as his deputy. Soon it seemed more appropriate to call these men Ironsides rather than Roundheads.

The Royalist strategy in the spring of 1645 was to thrust north through Worcester to Chester and then pick up reinforcements in the north, where there would still be plenty of sympathizers in spite of the disaster of Marston Moor the previous year. Rupert and Maurice cleared the way by victories at Ledbury and Chester, but Charles was slow to move.

Meanwhile, Cromwell, who was enjoying his first independent command, was sent to the Midlands to upset any Royalist plans. He lost no time in showing his ability and determination. He defeated the Earl of Northampton near Islip, compelled the surrender of Bletchington House, took 200 prisoners in a battle at Bampton, and made a vigorous though unsuccessful attack on Faringdon Castle. However, he could not prevent Charles leaving Oxford with an army numbering 11,000.

Both armies now began manœuvring for advantage. Fairfax came up from the west and threatened Oxford; Rupert countered the move by capturing and sacking Leicester. Charles, although aware that his army was large and well balanced, was not prepared to risk it in the open against vastly superior numbers. He therefore moved to Daventry and deliberated how he could relieve Oxford.

Fairfax, however, was aware that he had the initiative. On 12 June he broke off the investment of Oxford and moved swiftly to Kislingbury, eight miles east of Daventry. This was close enough to Charles to clash with the outposts. Charles had no intention of being forced to fight at a disadvantage on ground not of his own choosing and he retreated that night to Market Harborough. This move put him within reasonable reach of his base at Newark.

But Fairfax was hot on his heels. He reached Guilsborough, four miles south of Naseby, the next day. The news surprised the King and he saw that it was necessary to give battle. The position was by no means unsuitable. Two miles south of Market Harborough was a ridge of high ground covering the two miles from East Farndon to Great Oxendon, from the B.4036 to the A.508. Charles deployed his army along this position by 8 a.m. on 14 June.

Fairfax, following, breasted the Naseby ridge four miles south, and realized that this was going to be a major battle. He noted that the ground between Naseby and Clipston was marshy. If he could persuade Rupert to charge over it and up the ridge, this would be a good start for the day. Rupert, of course, had his eyes just as wide open as Fairfax and instead veered right on to the line of the Sibbertoft–Naseby road.

Fairfax saw Rupert's counter-move and promptly began to close left to meet it. This peculiar manœuvre shifted the battlefront one mile west of the original line. The area between them was now bounded by Dust Hill to the north, Red Hill to the south, and Sulby to the west. The centre was Broadmoor. The battlefield monument (*not* the Naseby obelisk) is just below Red Hill to the left of the road.

By 10 a.m. the armies were in their new position. On the Royalist side, Rupert commanded the cavalry on the right wing, Lord Astley had the foot in the centre, and Langdale took the cavalry on the left. The front was approximately a mile long. There was very little artillery on the Royalist side, as most had been left in the previous position. Opposite, Cromwell commanded the cavalry on the right, Skippon the centre foot, and Ireton the cavalry on the left. Cromwell also stationed 1000 dragoons on the left behind Sulby hedges under the command of Okey; these were in advance of the main Ironside line. (This was a similar disposition to Edward IV at the battle of Tewkesbury.) The Ironsides had all their guns.

Rupert began the battle with a typical charge, and Astley's foot were closing rapidly at the same time. Rupert aimed at the centre of Ireton's position but Ireton's men veered somewhat to the right. A flank attack by Okey's dragoons did nothing to stop him; he charged right into Ireton's left, and then settled down to cut and thrust with the sword. This was a tough, bloody period, but the Royalists got the better of it and forced a way through. Rupert was then able to regroup. Looking for another target, he decided to press on, but this move achieved little, for there were only the baggage-wagons to attack and what happened there could not affect the present battle. However, Rupert was careful not to waste too much time – not wanting to be accused of another Edgehill – but his absence from the field at this time was disastrous for his side.

In the centre the Royalist infantry had begun well and were forcing the Ironsides back. In attacking Ireton, Rupert, though pushing back the left wing, had left the right half and its commander intact. Ireton now used this part to attack Astley on the flank, as the latter's magnificent foot stormed up the hill. This was not intolerable for the Royalist foot but it was unwelcome. Even less welcome was the arrival of Okey's dragoons, who now advanced in a cavalry charge. Meanwhile, Cromwell had launched a tremendous cavalry charge on to Langdale's cavalry who were finding their way over the broken ground at the foot of the hill. It was full of rabbit-holes and bushes, and anyone caught there would be at a disadvantage. Cromwell needed only to use his leading regiments to wreak havoc in this area, but even these he was able to recall when their work was done. In the rear, he still had uncommitted troops.

This became the turning point of the battle. As Astley's infantry fought their way up Red Hill Ridge encountering no mean resistance from Skippon's foot, they received not only the shock of Ireton and Okey but now a tremendous blow on the other flank from Cromwell's cavalry. Even the forward units, who had ridden down Langdale, were turned back into the fight, and the second and third lines went in completely fresh.

At this point Rupert came back to the field, but with his horses blown could do no more than be a spectator. The sight he saw was enough to sicken anyone, heroic though it was. Astley's infantry, having fought their way up the ridge, having been attacked on three sides, were now being forced down again. They fought to the last, and were wiped out almost to a man – 4000 of them. Many of the cavalry fought it out to the end too, although it could not affect the result. But finally, with the King and Rupert gone, those who could tried to leave the field.

As on all battlefields the scenes of the heaviest fighting may be traced by names or grave pits. Red Hill Ridge and Red Hill Farm need no explanation.

This was probably the most decisive battle of the war and Charles should never have fought it. He was outnumbered by two to one, 14,000 to 7000, and he was short of cavalry.

Added to that, Rupert once again moved off the field in the wrong direction after an initial success. And the hard fact is that the Royalists probably underrated their opponents and paid dearly for it.

THE BATTLE OF
WORCESTER

3 September 1651

Cromwell called the Battle of Worcester the 'crowning mercy';
others might have had a different name for it.

It occurred six years after Naseby, that great, decisive but
badly-managed battle which had sealed the fate of the Royalist
cause. After it, Charles was little more than a fugitive, though
for a time it seemed as if he might once again turn the tables
with the help of Montrose. But in September 1645 Montrose
was defeated at Philiphaugh. There was still an army in the
west of England but this too was beaten by Fairfax at Lang-
port in September 1645, and from then onwards the Royalists
were forced westward until they surrendered in the spring of
1646. In April 1646, after watching his enemies gather round
Oxford for what would surely be the last and most fateful
siege of the war, Charles slipped away and surrendered to the
Scottish Covenanters who were then in camp at Newark.
He felt that it might be easier to make a deal with the Scots
than the English Parliament, but he was mistaken. The Scots
were adamant that he must make Presbyterianism the religion
of England – a stipulation which was quite unacceptable to
Charles. The Scots would have none of his temporizing and
abruptly handed him over to his English opponents.

Still Charles felt he could save something from the
wreckage. There was an apparently irreconcilable conflict
between the Presbyterians, who held the majority in Parliament, and the Independents, who drew the line at a state-
imposed religion. Cromwell and Fairfax supported the
Independents, as did the New Model Army as a whole. When
the Presbyterians tried to dismiss the New Model, which they
saw as the mainstay of the opposition, it refused to disperse.
Instead it marched to London and seized power.

The Independents then offered Charles moderate terms but

unwisely he refused them. He escaped to the Isle of Wight where he was kept under surveillance at Carisbrooke. He had long been negotiating – some would say intriguing – for a last uprising, and now it came. But it failed. In three months Cromwell and Fairfax had suppressed it. The last decisive battle was at Preston in 1648.

Charles was now sent to Hurst Castle, from which he could not escape. In January 1649, a packed High Court tried the King and condemned him to death; Charles refused to try to defend himself.

He was executed in Whitehall on 16 January 1649, meeting his death with exemplary courage and dignity.

A republic was now proclaimed but peace was still far away. First there was a mutiny amongst the army Cromwell was about to take to Ireland; then followed his relentless campaign against Irish resistance which is still a vivid and bitter memory in parts of Ireland to this day.

But the Scots had not struck their final blow. A new army was raised to fight for the cause of Prince Charles, later to be Charles II. Cromwell defeated it at Dunbar in September 1650 and went on to overrun the Lowlands and much of central Scotland.

It seemed all over, but it was not. In 1651 when Cromwell was at Perth, he learnt that Prince Charles had slipped past him and was marching rapidly down through England, picking up reinforcements on the way. It was a critical moment. There was no army between the Prince (he had in fact been crowned as Charles II at Scone) and London. However, he gained few recruits on his southerly march and lost many Scots from desertion. He decided therefore to pause at Worcester and let supporters come in from Wales and other areas which had for so long stood firmly by his father. Ironically, he set up his standard in Worcester nine years exactly after his father had set up his standard at Nottingham – on 22 August. Coincidentally, Cromwell marched into Nottingham on the very same day.

With 15,000 men only, in the heart of a hostile country, the future did not look very promising to Prince Charles.

Cromwell, by forced marching south, was now closing in on him. By the time Cromwell reached Evesham, sixteen miles from Worcester, he had 30,000 men, and his army was still growing. He had quite clear in his mind what he had to do, and was quite ruthless. The Royalist army must not merely be beaten but completely and finally destroyed. To accomplish this he must surround it and block every avenue of escape. This he now proceeded to do.

The subsequent battle took place in the fields north of Powick Bridge. The Severn runs north-south through Worcester, but to the south of the city it is joined by the Teme. Charles stationed his army on the north bank of the Teme and destroyed all nearby bridges on the Teme and Severn. This put him in the apex of a triangle and presumably he expected to inflict very heavy casualties on the Cromwellians who tried to cross the river to get at him. The Severn, being swift, deep and forty yards across, was likely to be of great assistance in this. The Teme, although only ten feet wide, was also ten feet deep and fast-flowing. It looked like being a difficult time for the Cromwellians.

Cromwell decided on a triple attack. He spent several days collecting boats from up and down the river, and, of course, they were there to be had in abundance. Several of the largest of these were towed upstream to a point where they could be made into bridging pontoons. One of these was to be used to cross the Teme with 11,000 men, the other to bridge the Severn. There was one further target to be attacked. This was Fort Royal outside the east wall of the town. It formed the rear headquarters of the Royalist position.

The southern party (under Fleetwood) approached the Teme with difficulty. Charles had left a rearguard on the south bank and it fought a strong delaying action around Powick Church.

Miraculously both 'bridges' seem to have been a success, though perhaps some of Fleetwood's men appear to have swum across or forded higher up. Cromwell's contingent is said to have crossed the Severn first, although in planning it was meant to come in on the second phase of the attack. Both reached the meadows, and there, step by bloody step, they pushed the Royalists back to St John's.

Charles seems to have encouraged his troops in the early phase of the battle and then ascended the cathedral tower to direct operations from that observation point. Seeing Cromwell's army now in two sections, with no chance of joining up again quickly, he decided to put in a swift counter-attack on that part of Cromwell's army which was still east of the Severn. He wasted no time. Personally leading the attack, with every soldier he could collect at short notice, he delivered a tremendous blow on the troops Cromwell had not yet committed to battle. He swept all before him and reached the eminence known as Red Hill.

With a less able opponent than Cromwell this counter-attack might have turned the battle. Cromwell, however, was not the man to relinquish a gain. Coming back across the bridge he hurled his troops into what he sensed was the key area of the conflict. Three hours bitter fighting followed. Only when Charles could no longer rally the Scottish cavalry to keep up their attack was the battle decided. Then, as darkness fell, panic raced through the Royalist ranks. The cavalry – or what was left of them – galloped off and left the infantry to their fate. The unfortunate foot had no chance at all; many were taken prisoner but most were killed. But they did not stop fighting; in some parts the struggle went on well into the night. Few of those who managed to escape from the battle-field were able to reach safety. It was a complete, devastating and final Roundhead victory. And it was, at last, the end of the Civil War.

APPENDICES

1 ASSER'S ACCOUNT OF
THE BATTLE OF ASHDOWN

Asser's account seems to be a combination of rhetoric, fact and surmise. This is hardly surprising, for it was one of many battles, and even if Alfred discussed it personally it is probable that he had some difficulty in recalling exactly what occurred.

. . . In the next year (869) was there a mighty famine, and death among men, and plague among beasts. And the aforesaid Heathen host rode back to the Northumbrians and came to the city of York, and there abode one whole year. And in the next year (870) they made their way through Mercia to East Anglia, and in a place called Theodford [Thetford] they wintered. In this same year Edmund, King of the East Angles, fought against that same host a desperate fight. But, also, the Heathen won all too gloriously; and there was he slain, and the most of his men with him; and they held the death-stead, and brought beneath their sway all that land.

And in the same year did Archbishop Ceolnoth, the Bishop of Dorobernia [Canterbury], go the way of all flesh, and in that city was he buried in peace.

But in the year of our Lord's Incarnation 871, and the 22nd of the age of King Alfred, did that Heathen host, hateful to tell, leave the East Angles, and hied them to the realm of the West Saxons, and came unto a town royal, called Rædig [Reading], which lieth on the bank of Thames-stream River [*Tamesis flumensis fluminis*] to the south, in that part which is called Bearrocscire. And on the third day of their coming thither, then rode forth their chiefs, and many with them, to harry the land; and the rest were after making them a dyke between the two rivers, Thames and Cynetan [Kennet], on the right hand [i.e. to the south; until the sixteenth century the East, not the North, was the top of the map] of that town royal.

Then did Ethelwulf, Alderman of the land of Berkshire, with his comrades, cross their path at the place called Englefield; and there fought both sides full valiantly, and long did either stand their ground. Of the two Heathen captains the one was slain, and the most part of that host laid low. Then fled away the rest, and the Christians gat them the victory, and held the death-stead. Yet four days more, after this hap, and there came Ethelred, King of the West Saxons, and Alfred his brother, and joined forces, and gathered them a host, and drew nigh unto Reading, cutting down and overthrowing whomsoever of the Heathen they found without the stronghold, and made their way even unto the gates. No less keen in fight were the Heathen. Out they burst from every gate like wolves; and then waxed long the fight, and ever more deadly. But, alas, alas, in the end did the Christians turn their backs, and the Heathen gat them the victory and held the death-stead. And there, amongst the rest, fell the above-named Alderman, Ethelwulf.

Stirred by this woe and shame, the Christians, after yet another four days, went forth to battle against the aforesaid host, at a place called Æscesdun [Ashdown] (which in Latin is by interpretation Ash Mount), with their whole strength, and with a good will. But the Heathen formed in two divisions, of like size, made ready their shield-wall [*testudo*]. For they had, as at that time, two Kings and many Chieftains; and the one half of their army gave they unto the two Kings, and the rest unto all the Chieftains together. And when the Christians saw this, they too, in like manner, parted their host in twain, and as keenly formed their shield-wall.

But Alfred, with his men, as we have heard from truthful eye-witnesses, came the quicker to the field and more readily. Nor wonder was it; for his brother King Ethelred was still in his tent, fixed in prayer, hearing Mass. For ever would he say that never while he lived would he leave his Mass before the Priest had ended it, nor, for any man on earth, turn his back on Divine Service. And even so he did. And much availed with the Lord the faith of that Christian King, as in what followeth will appear most plainly.

The Christians, then, had thought best that Ethelred the King, with his force, should take battle against the two Kings of the Heathen; while Alfred his brother, with his band, should be told, as was meet, to chance the fight [*belli sumere sortem*] against all the Heathen Chieftains. And when thus on either side they were in good order, and the King tarried long in prayer, Alfred, then second in command, could stand the advance of the foe no longer. Needs must be either draw him back from the battle, or charge the enemy ere yet his brother came into the fray. And, at the last, in manly wise, charged he with the rush of a wild boar, leading his Christian forces against the foemen's hosts, even as had been fore-planned (save only that the King was not yet come), for he trusted in God's counsel and leant upon His aid. So drew he together his shield-wall in good order, and advanced his banner straight against the foe.

But here those who know not the place must be told that it was no fair field of battle, for the Heathen had seized the higher ground, and the Christian battle-line was charging uphill. There was also in that same place a lone thorn-tree and a low, which we ourselves have beheld. Around this, then, came the lines together, with a mighty shouting, in warrior wise, the one side bent upon all mischief [*perperam agentes*], the other to fight for life and land and dear ones. This way and that swayed the battle for a while, valiant was it and all too deadly, till so God ordered it that the Heathen could stand against the Christian charge no longer. Most part of their force were slain, and with all shame they betook them to flight.

And in that place fell there by the sword one of the two

Heathen Kings, and of their Chieftains five, and many a thousand of their men beside them. Yea, and, moreover, thousands more, scattered over the whole breadth of the field of Ashdown, were cut to pieces far and wide. And there then fell there Bægsceg their King, and Sidroc the Elder, their Chieftain, and Sidroc the Younger, their Chieftain, and Osbern the Chieftain, and Frena the Chieftain, and Harold the Chieftain. And the whole Heathen host fled them away all that day and all that night, even unto the next day; till they that escaped got back into their stronghold. And even until nightfall held the Christians the chase, and smote them down on every side.

And after this, again fourteen days, Ethelred the King and Alfred his brother, with their united force, hied them to Basing to fight against the Heathen. There joined they battle, and stood to it long. But the Heathen gained the day and held the field. And when this fray was lost and won, came there from over sea yet another Heathen host and joined the horde. And in the same year, after Easter, Ethelred, the aforesaid King, after ruling his realm well and worshipfully amid many a trouble, went the way of all flesh, and is buried in the monastery at Wimborne, where he awaiteth the Coming of the Lord and the First Resurrection with the just.

In the same year did our Alfred (who until then, while his brothers lived, had been in the second place) take upon him, so soon as ever his brother was dead, the sway of the whole kingdom, by the grant of God, and with all goodwill of the land-folk, one and all. For even while his brother was yet alive might he eftsoon have won it, would he have taken it, and that with the assent of all men: seeing that both in wisdom and eke in all good ways was he better than all his brethren put together — yea, and, in especial, a surpassing warrior, and, in war, had ever almost the best of it. Then began he to reign, as it were unwillingly. For it seemed unto him that never might he, all alone, with but God for aid, endure so grievous a stress and strain of heathendom; whenas, even along with his brothers, while they lived, full hardly and with great loss might he abide it.

So reigned he one full month, and thereafter, on the hill called Wilton, on the southern bank of the river Guilou [Willy] (from which river the whole of that shire is named), fought he, with but few behind him, against the whole Heathen host, a fight all too unequal. Up and down most part of the day raged the fight stoutly. Then were the eyes of the Heathen opened, and they saw to the full their peril. And therewith bore they up no longer against their unremitting foe, but turned their backs and fled away. But, alas, through the rashness of the pursuit they tricked us. On they came again to battle, and won the victory, and were masters of the death-stead.

2 LUDLOW'S ACCOUNT OF
THE BATTLE OF EDGEHILL

Edmund Ludlow's account of Edgehill is noteworthy, for the majority of descriptions of the battle are from the Royalist viewpoint. This one comes from the opposite side.

. . . The night following [Powick Bridge] the enemy left Worcester, and retreated to Shrewsbury, where the King was; upon which the Earl of Essex advanced to Worcester, where he continued with the army for some time, expecting an answer to a message sent by him to the King from the Parliament, inviting him to return to London. This time the King improved to compleat and arm his men; which when he had effected, he began his march, the Earl of Essex attending him to observe his motions; and after a day or two, on Sunday morning, the 23rd of October, 1642, our scouts brought advice that the enemy appeared, and about nine o'clock some of their troops were discovered upon Edge-hill in Warwickshire. Upon this our forces, who had been order'd that morning to their quarters to refresh themselves, having had but little rest for eight and forty hours, were immediately counter-manded. The enemy drew down the hill, and we went into the field near Keinton. The best of our field-pieces were planted upon our right wing, guarded by two regiments of foot, and some horse. Our general having commanded to fire upon the enemy, it was done twice upon that part of the army wherein, as it was reported, the King was. The great shot was exchanged on both sides for the space of an hour or thereabouts. By this time the foot began to engage, and a party of the enemy being sent to line some hedges on our right wing, thereby to beat us from our ground, were repulsed by our dragoons without any loss on our side. The enemy's body of foot, wherein the King's standard was, came on with musquet-shot of us; upon which we observing no horse to encounter withal, charged then with some loss from their pikes, tho very little from their shot; but not being able to break them, we retreated to our former station, whither we were no sooner come, but we perceived that those who were appointed to guard the artillery were marched off; and Sir Philip Stapylton, our captain, wishing for a regiment of foot to secure the cannon, we promised to stand by him in defence of them, causing one of our servants to load and level one of them, which he had scarce done, when a body of horse appeared advancing towards us from that side where the enemy was. We fired at them with case-shot, but did no other mischief save only wounding one man through the hand, our gun being overloaded, and planted on high ground; which fell out very happily, this body of horse being of our own army, and commanded by Sir William Balfour, who with great resolution had charged into the enemy's quarters, where he had nailed several pieces of their cannon, and was then retreating to his own party, of which the man who was shot in the hand was giving us notice by holding it up; but we did not discern it. The Earl of Essex order'd two regiments of foot to attack that body which we had charged before, where the King's standard was, which they did, but could not break them till Sir William Balfour at the head of a party of horse charging them in the rear, and we marching down to take them in the flank,

they brake and ran away towards the hill. Many of them
were killed upon the place, amongst whom was Sir Edward
Varney the King's standard-bearer, who, as I have heard
from a person of honour, engaged on that side, not out of
any good opinion of the cause, but from the sense of duty
which he thought lay upon him, in respect of his relation
to the King. Mr [William] Herbert of Glamorganshire,
Lieutenant Colonel to Sir Edward Stradling's regiment,
was also killed, with many others that fell in the pursuit.
Many colours were taken, and I saw Lieutenant Colonel
Middleton, then a reformado in our army, displaying the
King's standard which he had taken; but a party of horse
coming upon us, we were obliged to retire with our
standard; and having brought it to the Earl of Essex, he
delivered it to the custody of one Mr [Robert] Chambers,
his secretary, from whom it was taken by one Captain
[John] Smith, who, with two more, disguising themselves
with orange-colour'd scarfs (the Earl of Essex's colour), and
pretending it unfit that a penman should have the honour
to carry the standard, took it from him, and rode with it
to the King, for which action he was knighted. Retreating
towards our army, I fell in with a body of the King's foot,
as I soon perceived; but having passed by them undiscovered, I met with Sir William Balfour's troop, some of
whom who knew me not would have fired upon me,
supposing me to be an enemy, had they not been prevented,
and assured of the contrary by Mr Francis Russell, who
with ten men well mounted and armed, which he maintained, rode in the lifeguard, and in the heat of the pursuit
had lost sight of them, as I myself had also done.

I now perceived no other engagement on either side, only
a few great guns continued to fire upon us from the enemy:
but towards the close of the day we discovered a body of
horse marching from our rear on the left of us under the
hedges, which the life-guard (whom I had then found)
having discovered to be the enemy, and resolving to charge
them, sent to some of our troops that stood within musquet-
shot of us to second them; which though they refused to do,

and we had no way to come at them but through a gap in the hedge, we advanced towards them, and falling upon their reàr, killed divers of them, and brought off some arms. In which attempt being dismounted I could not without great difficulty recover on horse-back again, being loaded with cuirassier's arms, as the rest of the guard also were. This was the right wing of the King's horse commanded by Prince Rupert, who, taking advantage of the disorder that our own horse had put our foot into, who had opened their ranks to secure them in their retreat, pressed upon them with such fury, that he put them to flight. And if the time which he spent in pursueing them too far, and in plundering the wagons, had been employed in taking such advantages as offered themselves in the place where the fight was, it might have proved more serviceable to the carrying on of the enemy's designs. The night after the battle our army quartered upon the same ground that the enemy fought on the day before. No man nor horse got any meat that night, and I had touched none since the Saturday before, neither could I find my servant who had my cloak, so that having nothing to keep me warm but a suite of iron, I was obliged to walk about all night, which proved very cold by reason of a sharp frost.

3   RELICS OF THE BATTLE OF EDGEHILL

Brigadier Peter Young, DSO, MC, who is the most authoritative writer on Edgehill, has kindly allowed me to quote the following notes on relics of the battle.

In July 1967 Miss M. Fell of 58 Keswick Walk, Wyken, Coventry, presented three lead musket balls to the author. These were picked up on the battlefield some 80 years ago by her grandfather, a Mr Hemming, a native of Kineton – of the family of John Hemming or Hemminge (d. 1630), actor and co-editor of the first folio of Shakespeare. Two of the bullets weigh 1¾ oz. and the other 1⅛ oz. The line round the circumference caused by the bullet mould can be clearly seen on the two heavier bullets. The author has a bullet from Marston Moor which weighs just over an ounce, and five from Naseby, one of which weighs fractionally more than an ounce, and the others just under. During a search of the Gravesend Copse area, using mine detectors, a leaden musket ball, weighing approximately 1¼ oz., was found (1967).

Another bullet, given to a Mr Prickett, and now in the possession of David Fisher, was weighed in the author's presence (6 August 1967) and found to be 2 lb. 14¾ oz. In theory a minion was a 4-pounder and a falcon a 2¼-pounder. This bullet would be too large for the latter, and would have made a very inaccurate projectile for the former; fitting the barrel very badly and therefore having altogether too much 'windage' it would wander in its flight. It was picked up at Moorlands Farm and must, therefore, have been discharged by the Parliamentarian artillery. A similar ball was found at Hornton by a Mr Yates.

On 5 August Mr T. Jeffes of Radway showed the author two cannon-balls given to him by a Mr Griffin in 1964. These came from the Thistleton Farm area and had been taken thence in about 1941, when the War Department took over. They weigh approximately 23½ lb. and 12 lb. respectively, from which one would conclude that they were fired by a demi-cannon and a culverin respectively. One would expect that balls found in the Thistleton Farm area would be from the Royalist guns. Certainly they had two demi-cannon – theoretically 27-pounders – and two culverins – theoretically 15-pounders. The Parliamentarians lost two 12-pounders in the battle, and it is not impossible that the second bullet was ammunition for one of them.

Mr Martin Jeffes showed the author a musket bullet similar to those sent him by Miss Fell. He had discovered this (c. 1963) while ditching about a quarter of a mile NW of the present Radway Church. This could be a Parliamentarian bullet fired during the last phase of the battle.

A ball weighing 19 pounds and two others weighing only half a pound each, are in the possession of Lord Leycester Hospital, Warwick. They were found near Thistleton Farm and should therefore be Royalist missiles. The three small balls may be caseshot, but they could have been fired from a robinet, which was a $\frac{3}{4}$-pounder.

During the construction of the Central Ammunition Depot, Kineton (1942), six or more cannon balls were found in the vicinity of the Graveyard. Their weight is said to have varied from 6 to 22 pounds, but it seems that their exact weight and precise location were not properly recorded and so this proves very little.

In 1922, during the construction of the Ironstone Railway from Edgehill to Kineton, some cannon-balls were found in a disused brick-kiln at a point described as 300 yards east along the Arlescote Road from the foot of Bullet Hill. These must have been some of the shots from Ramsey's wing which, as Bulstrode tells us, 'mounted over our Troops, without doing any Hurt . . .'

Other relics of the battle include hand-made nails, a seventeenth century horseshoe and part of the rim tyre of a heavy vehicle found during the mine detector search of Great Grounds (1967), a spear (pike?) head found by Mr Yates of Hornton, and a pikehead found at Upland Farm in 1950, and now in the Banbury Museum. The same museum possesses a sword found in Broughton Churchyard, while Mr L. Todd of Manor Farm, Ratley, found another sword in 1950. Grimmer remains were found in about 1880 near the ford on the Little Kineton to Kineton road: the skeletons of several men, perhaps Parliamentarian runaways, or men detailed to escort the baggage train.

One is struck by the fact that a number of these cannon balls do not fit neatly into the various types of artillery used in 1642. One would expect to find 27- or 15-pound balls for demi-cannon and culverin, yet we find balls of $23\frac{1}{2}$, 22 and 19 pounds. It is evident that theory and practice did not go hand in hand. Yet this is not so surprising when we recall the charges of inefficiency levelled against

the Parliamentarian artillery, and the difficulties of the
Royalists in providing a train at all. Their troubles are
illustrated by a petition recently found in the Public Record
Office by Dr Ian Roy:

When his late Matie: was to take the feilde, the firste
Councell of war appointed Sr John Heydon Sr John
Pennington Sr Bryan Palmes Sr George Strode and John
Wandesforde to forme and conduct the traine of Artillery
att Edge hill, Sr George received woundes which were
helde mortall, and John Wandesforde alone brought of
the trayne to Oxforde and his Highenesse Prince Ruperte
did Commaunde dragoones to dismounte and Imployed
those in that Saruice.

(SP.29.66. No. 46)

One can only admire the Prince's talent for improvisa-
tion. The comments of the dragoons are best left to the
readers' imagination.

4 ACCOUNTS OF THE SIEGES OF
HEREFORD AND COLCHESTER

Mention has been made in the text of various sieges. Many
of these were battles in miniature and even more demanding.
Here we reproduce two examples: an account of Hereford,
as described in a letter to the Lord Digby from the Governor
(reproduced by kind permission of Mrs C. M. F. Parsons);
and of Colchester, in the second phase of the battle, from the
Beaufort manuscripts.

My Lord,
    A Numerous and Active Army close besieging us hath
rendred me, and those engaged with me, (in regard of
perpetuall duty, without reliefe of Guards for five weeks
together) incapable of presenting your Lordship with an
exact Relation thereof: I can therefore hint it only for a

better Mercury. The Officers, Gentry, (whereof I shall send a list) Clergy, Citizens, and Common Souldiers, behaved themselves all gallantly upon their duty, many eminently; to particularise each, would be too great a trespasse on your Lordships more weighty affaires. Briefly beleeve me (my Lord) the walls of their valiant breasts were all strongly lined with Courage and Loyalty.

On the 30th of July, I sent out a party of 20 Horse over Wye-bridge, who discovering their Forlorne-hope of horse, charged them into their maine Body; and retreated in very little disorder, and with losse only of one Trooper, (taken prisoner) some of the Scots falling. Immediatly after this, their whole Body of Horse faced us, about ten of the Clock in the morning within the reach of our Cannon, and were welcomed with our mettall; good execution being done upon them, their Foot as yet undiscovered. About halfe an houre after, I caused a strong Party of Foot (seconded with Horse) to line the hedges, who galled them in their passage to the Fords, after whose handsome retreat, I began to ensafe the Ports, which I did that night. In the morning, appeared their Body of Foot, and we found our selves surrounded. I injoyned the Bells silence, least their ringing, which was an Alarme to awaken our devotion, might Chime them together to the execution of their malice. For the same reason, I stopt our Clocks, and hereby though I prevented their telling tales, to the advantage of the Enemy, I myselfe lost the punctuall observation of many particulars, which therefore I must more confusedly represent unto your Lordship.

Before they attempted any thing against the Towne, they invited us to a Surrendry, and this they did by a double Summons, one from Leven, directed to me; the other from the Committee of both Kingdomes (attending on the affaires of the Army) sent to the Major and Corporation: but we complyed so well in our Resolutions, that our positive answer served for both Parties, which was returned by me to their Generall.

This not giving that satisfaction they desired, they began

to approach upon the first of August, but very slowly and modestly; as yet intending more the security of their owne persons, then the ruine of ours: but all their Art could not protect them from our small and great shot which fell upon them. Besides this, our men galled them handsomly at their severall Sallies, over Wyebridge, once beat them up to their maine guard, and at another demolisht one side of St Martins Steeple; which would have much annoyed us at the Bridge and Pallace; this was performed with the hurt only of two men, but with losse of great store of the Enemies men.

When they saw how difficult the Service would prove, before they could compasse their designes by force, they made use of another Engine which was flattery. The Major and Aldermen are courted to yeeld the Towne by an Epistle, subscribed by six of the Country Gentlemen, very compassionate and suasory: but upon our refusall to stoup to this lure, they were much incensed that they had been so long disappointed, and having all this while continued their line of Communication, they raised their Batteries, commencing at Wyebridge, from whence they received the greatest dammage, but instead of revenging that losse upon us, they multiplied their owne, by the death of their much lamented Major Generall Crafford, and some others that fell with him. This provoked them to play hot upon the Gate for two days together, and battered it so much, (being the weakest) that it was rendered uselesse, yet our men stopt it up with Wooll-sacks and Timber, and for our greater assurance of eluding their attempt, we brake an Arch, and raised a very strong Worke behind it.

The Enemy frustrate of his hopes here, raiseth two severall Batteries, one at the Fryers, the other on the other side of Wye River, and from both these, playes his Ordinance against the corner of the wall by Wye side, but we repaire and line our walls faster then they can batter them, whereupon they desist.

About the 11th of August, we discover a Mine at Freingate, and imploy workmen to countermine them. When we had stopt the progresse of that Mine on one side of the Gate, they carried it on the other; which we also defeated by making a Sally-Port: and issuing forth did break it open and fire it.

About the 13th, they raise Batteries round about the Town, and make a Bridge over Wye River.

The 14th, Doctor Scudamore is sent by them to desire admittance for three Country Gentlemen, who pretended in their Letters to import something of consequence to the good of the City and County, free leave of ingresse and egresse was allowed them, but being admitted, their suggestions were found to us so frivolous and impertinent, that they were dismisd not without some disrelish and neglect: and the said Doctor, after they were past the Port, comming back from his company, was unfortunately slaine by a shot from the Enemy.

About the 16th, they discover the face of their Battery against Frein-gate, with five severall gun-ports, from hence they played foure Cannon joyntly at our walls, and made a breach, which was instantly made up; they doe the like on the other side with the like successe.

The 17th, a notable Sally was made at St Owens Church with great execution, and divers Prisoners taken with the losse only of one man, at which time little boyes strived, which should first carry Torches and Faggots to fire their works, which was performed to some purpose, and so it was at the same Sally-port once before, though with a fewer number, and therefore with lesse execution.

And I may not forget to acquaint your Lordship with those other foure Sallies, made by us at the Castle to good effect, and what emulation there was between the Souldier and Citizens, which should be most ingaged in them: Now their losse of Prisoners, slaughter of men, and dishonour of being beaten out of their works, which they found ready to flame about their eares if they returned presently into them, had so kindled their indignation, that presently they raysed Batteries against Saint Owens Church, and plaid fiercely at it, but to little purpose, which they so easily perceived, that from the 20, unto the 27, there was a great calme on all sides, we as willing to provide ourselves, and preserve our ammunition for a storme, as they could be industrious or malitious to bring it upon us: yet I cannot say either side was Idle; for they ply'd their Mine at Saint Owens, and prepared for Scaling, we countermined, imploy'd our boyes by day and night to steale out and fire their Works, securing their retreat under the protection of our Musquetiers upon the wall, and what our fire could not perfect, though it burnt farre, and suffocated some of their Miners, our water did, breaking in upon them and drowning that which the fire had not consumed, and this saved us the pains of pursuing a mine, which we had sunk on purpose to render theirs in that place ineffectuall.

The 29th, Leven (a mercifull Generall) assayes the Towne againe by his last offer of honourable conditions to surrender, but he found us still unrelenting, the terror of his Cannon, making no impression at all upon our Spirits, though the bullets discharged from them, had done so much against our walls: this (though some of their chiefe Commanders were remisse and coole at the debate and some contradictory) drives their greatest spirits into a passionate resolution of storming.

And to that purpose August 31th, and September 1. they prepare Ladders, hurdles, and other accommodations for the advancing their designe, and secuting their persons in the attempt, and played very hot with their Cannon upon Bysters gate, and the halfe moon next Saint Owens gate, intending the morrow after to fall on, presuming as they boasted, that after they had rung us this passing peale, they should presently force the Garrison to give up her Loyall Ghost, but the same night His Majesty advancing from Worcester, gave them a very hot alarum, and drawing a little neerer to us, like the Sunne to the Meridian, this Scottish mist beganne to disperse, and the next morning vanished out of sight. My Lord, I should give your Lordship an accompt of the valor of our common Souldiers and Townesmen, that would hazard themselves at the making up of breaches (to the astonishment of the Enemy) till their Cannon played between their leggs, and even the Women (such was their gallantry) ventred where the Musquet bullets did so, and I should acquaint your Honour, what frequent alarums we gave them by fire-balls, lights upon our Steeple, by Dogs, Cats, and outworne Horses, having light Matches tyed about them; and turned out upon their works, whereby we put the enemy in such distraction, that sometimes they charged one another; this recreation we had in the middest of our besiedging: and one morning, instead of beating Reveillie, we had a crye of Hounds, in pursuit after the traine of a Fox about the Walls of the Citty, so little were we dismaied at the threats or attempts of them. I may not forget one remarkable peece of Divine providence, that God sent us singular men of all professions, very usefull, and necessary for us in this distresse, and so accidentally to us, as if they had on purpose been let downe from Heaven, to serve our present and emergent occasions; as skilfull Miners, excellent Cannoneers, (one whereof spent but one shot in vaine throughout the whole Siedge) an expert Carpenter, the only man in all the Country to make Mills, without whom we had been much disfurnisht of a meanes to make Powder (after our Powder-mill was burnt) or grind Corne; that providence that brought these to us, at last drove our Enemies from us, after the destruction of four or five Mines, which since appeares to be their number, the expence of 300 Cannon shot, besides other Ammunition spent with Muskets, the losse by their owne confession of 1200, and as the Country sayes 2000 men, we in all not loosing about 21 by all Casualties whatsoever. Thus craving your Lordships pardon for my prolixity, I take leave and rest

Your Lordship's most humble servant
BER. SCUDAMORE.

Being cut off from our forage, and having no provision of hay and oats in the town, on Saturday the fifteenth of July, about ten at night, we attempted to break away with part of our horse, ordering them to march northward, and join with the Scotch Armie, who, as we were informed by private letters, were upon their march to our relief . . . But the enemy having blocked up all the passes, we failed in our attempt, which upon second thoughts we thankfully acknowledged to Providence preserving us against our design. For had the horse passed we had wanted their flesh, upon which we fed six weeks; and their riders whom as we ordered, made the strongest part of our defence; for as their horses were slaughtered for our provision, they were armed with halberds, brown bills, and scythes, straightened and fastened to handles, about six foot long, weapons which the enemy strongly apprehended, but rather of terror than use, for they required such distances to manage them, that they could not be brought to fight in a gross. These were divided into three companies and commanded by my Lord of Norwich, the Lord Capell, and Sir Charles Lucas, who took their posts and hutted themselves upon the line, where they fed and lodged with their souldiers, a wise and worthy undertaking to revive the antient discipline; for though we humbly confess our sins, the primary cause which hath pulled down these judgments upon us, yet we look upon our luxuries and remissness in discipline as the proximate causes of our ruin. For many of our general officers in the former wars had such indulgence for their debaucheries that they adopted none to preferments but the companions of their pleasures.

'The enemy began their approaches on the east part of the town, called Berrie fields, which we suffered with great silence from our cannon, for besides our want of ammunition we desired an assault, as the likeliest means of our relief; only to free us from surprise we were forced to fire some of the neighbouring houses of the suburbs, where the enemy might have lodged their whole army within pistol shot of our walls . . .

'The last month passed quietly, for the enemy knew that we must be reduced by our wants, and we allowed them to make their approaches unchecked for lack of ammunition.'

The besieged were at last compelled to reduce the allowance of bread to seven ounces a day. 'It was received without murmuring by the souldiers, though being made of mault, oats, and rye which had taken salt water, it was not only distasteful, but such unwholesome food, that many chose to eat their horse and dog's flesh without it. But the greater suffering was of the poor inhabitants, who were reduced to that extremity that they ate soape and candle, which they endured with notable resolution . . . But upon review of our magazine and the provisions of private families, we found our store so little, that it was thought fit time to send a letter to Fairfax, wherein we proposed that if he would grant a truce for twenty days, and a pass for a messenger to find out Sir Marmaduke Langdale, if we were informed that in that interim he were not in a condition to relieve us, then we would treat with him upon a surrender. But the insolent enemy refused it, whereupon we resolved to continue our defence, hoping that the justice of our cause and the temper of our proceedings might in some degree make us worthy of the protection of Providence and our friends.'

5 ACCOUNTS OF LANSDOWN AND SECOND NEWBURY FROM CLARENDON'S 'HISTORY'

From Clarendon's *History of the Rebellion* I have taken accounts of the Battle of Lansdown and the Second Battle of Newbury. The book was begun in 1646 but not published until 1702; his battle descriptions are extremely vivid.

These extracts appear by courtesy of the Oxford University Press, who hold perpetual copyright on Clarendon's work.

After this disposition, and eight or ten days' rest at Wells, the army generally expressing a cheerful impatience to meet with the enemy, of which, at that time, they had a greater contempt, than in reason they should have; the

prince and marquis advanced to Frome, and thence to
Bradford, within four miles of Bath. And now no day
passed without action, and very sharp skirmishes; sir
William Waller having received from London a fresh
regiment of five hundred horse, under the command of
sir Arthur Haslerig: which were so completely armed, that
they were called by the other side the regiment of lobsters,
because of their bright iron shells, with which they were
covered, being perfect cuirassiers; and were the first seen
so armed on either side, and the first that made any impression upon the king's horse; who, being unarmed, were not
able to bear a shock with them; besides that they were
secure from hurts of the sword, which were almost the only
weapons the other were furnished with.

The contention was hitherto with parties; in which the
successes were various, and almost with equal losses: for
as sir William Waller, upon the first advance from Wells,
beat up a regiment of horse and dragoons of sir James
Hamilton's, and dispersed them; so, within two days, the
king's forces beat a party of his from a pass near Bath,
where the enemy lost two field-pieces, and near an hundred
men. But sir William Waller had the advantage in his
ground, having a good city, well furnished with provisions,
to quarter his army together in; and so in his choice not to
fight, but upon extraordinary advantage. Whereas the king's
forces must either disperse themselves, and so give the
enemy advantage upon their quarters, or, keeping near
together, lodge in the field, and endure great distress of
provision; the country being so disaffected, that only force
could bring in any supply or relief. Hereupon, after several
attempts to engage the enemy to a battle upon equal terms,
which, having the advantage, he wisely avoided; the
marquis and prince Maurice advanced with their whole
body to Marsfield, five miles beyond Bath towards Oxford;
presuming, that, by this means, they should draw the enemy
from their place of advantage, his chief business being to
hinder them from joining with the king. And if they had
been able to preserve that temper, and had neglected the

enemy, till he had quitted his advantages, it is probable they might have fought upon as good terms as they desired. But the unreasonable contempt they had of the enemy, and confidence they should prevail in any ground, together with the straits they endured for want of provisions, and their want of ammunition, which was spent as much in the daily hedge skirmishes, and upon their guards, being so near as could have been in battle, would not admit that patience; for sir William Waller, who was not to suffer that body to join with the king, no sooner drew out his whole army to Lansdown, which looked towards Marsfield, but they suffered themselves to be engaged upon great disadvantage.

It was upon the fifth of July when sir William Waller, as soon as it was light, possessed himself of that hill; and after he had, upon the brow of the hill over the high way, raised breastworks with fagots and earth, and planted cannon there, he sent a strong party of horse towards Marsfield, which quickly alarmed the other army, and was shortly driven back to their body. As great a mind as the king's forces had to cope with the enemy, when they had drawn into battalia, and found the enemy fixed on the top of the hill, they resolved not to attack them upon so great disadvantage; and so retired again towards their old quarters: which sir William Waller perceiving, sent his whole body of horse and dragoons down the hill, to charge the rear and flank of the king's forces; which they did throughly, the regiment of cuirassiers so amazing the horse they charged, that they totally routed them; and, standing firm and unshaken themselves, gave so great terror to the king's horse, who had never before turned from an enemy, that no example of their officers, who did their parts with invincible courage, could make them charge with the same confidence, and in the same manner they had usually done. However, in the end, after sir Nicholas Slanning, with three hundred musketeers, had fallen upon and beaten their reserve of dragooners, prince Maurice and the earl of Carnarvon, rallying their horse, and winging them with the Cornish musketeers, charged the enemy's horse again, and totally routed them; and in the same manner received two bodies more, and routed and chased them to the hill; where they stood in a place almost inaccessible. On the brow of the hill there were breast-works, on which were pretty bodies of small shot, and some cannon; on either flank grew a pretty thick wood towards the declining of the hill, in which strong parties of musketeers were placed; at the rear was a very fair plain, where the reserves of horse and foot stood ranged; yet the Cornish foot were so far from being appalled at this disadvantage, that they desired to fall on, and cried out, 'that they might have leave to fetch off those cannon'. In the end, order was given to attempt the hill with horse and foot. Two strong parties of musketeers were sent into the woods, which flanked the enemy; and the horse and other musketeers up the road way, which were charged by the enemy's horse, and routed; then sir Bevil Greenvil advanced with a party of horse, on his right hand, that ground being best for them; and his musketeers on the left; himself leading up his pikes in the middle; and in the face of their cannon, and small-shot from the breast-works, gained the brow of the hill, having sustained two full charges of the enemy's horse; but in the third charge his horse failing, and giving ground, he received, after other wounds, a blow on the head with a pole-axe, with which he fell, and many of his officers about him; yet the musketeers fired so fast upon the enemy's horse, that they quitted their ground, and the two wings, who were sent to clear the woods, having done their work, and gained those parts of the hill, at the same time beat off their enemy's foot, and became possessed of the breast-works; and so made way for their whole body of horse, foot, and cannon, to ascend the hill; which they quickly did, and planted themselves on the ground they had won; the enemy retiring about demi-culverin shot behind a stone wall upon the same level, and standing in reasonable good order.

Either party was sufficiently tired, and battered, to be contented to stand still. The king's horse were so shaken, that of two thousand which were upon the field in the morning, there were not above six hundred on the top of the hill. The enemy was exceedingly scattered too, and had no mind to venture on plain ground with those who had beaten them from the hill; so that, exchanging only some shot from their ordnance, they looked one upon another till the night interposed. About twelve of the clock, it being very dark, the enemy made a show of moving towards the ground they had lost; but giving a smart volley of small-shot, and finding themselves answered with the like, they made no more noise: which the prince observing, he sent a common soldier to hearken as near the place, where they were, as he could; who brought word, 'that the enemy had left lighted matches in the wall behind which they had lain, and were drawn off the field'; which was true; so that, as soon as it was day, the king's army found themselves possessed entirely of the field, and the dead, and all other ensigns of victory: sir William Waller being marched to Bath, in so much disorder and apprehension, that he left great store of arms, and ten barrels of powder, behind him; which was a very seasonable supply to the other side, who had spent in that days service no less than fourscore barrels, and had not a safe proportion left.

In this battle, on the king's part, there were more officers and gentlemen of quality slain, than common men; and more hurt than slain. That which would have clouded any victory, and made the loss of others less spoken of, was the death of sir Bevil Greenvil. He was indeed an excellent person, whose activity, interest, and reputation, was the foundation of what had been done in Cornwall; and his temper and affections so public, that no accident which happened could make any impressions in him; and his example kept other from taking any thing ill, or at least seeming to do so. In a word, a brighter courage, and a gentler disposition, were never married together to make the most cheerful and innocent conversation.

Very many officers and persons of quality were hurt; as the lord Arundel of Wardour, shot in the thigh with a brace of pistol bullets; sir Ralph Hopton, shot through the arm with a musket; sir George Vaughan, and many others, hurt in the head of their troops with swords and pole-axes; of which none of name died. But the morning added much to the melancholy of their victory, when the field was entirely their own. For sir Ralph Hopton riding up and down the field to visit the hurt men, and to put the soldiers in order, and readiness for motion, sitting on his horse, with other officers and soldiers about him, near a waggon of ammunition, in which were eight barrels of power; whether by treachery, or mere accident, is uncertain, the powder was blown up; and many, who stood nearest, killed; and many more maimed; among whom sir Ralph Hopton and sergent major Sheldon were miserably hurt.

Second Newbury

With his own, and the forces which had been under Essex, Major-general Philip Skippon fell upon the quarter at Speen, and passed the river; which was not well defended by the officer who was appointed to guard it with horse and foot, very many of them being gone off from their guards, as never imagining that they would, at that time of day, have attempted a quarter that was thought the strongest of all. But having thus got the river, they marched in good order, with very great bodies of foot, winged with horse, towards the heath; from whence the horse which were left there, with too little resistance, retired; being in truth much overpowered, by reason the major part of them, upon confidence of security of the pass, were gone to provide forage for their horse.

By this means the enemy possessed themselves of the ordnance which had been planted there, and of the village of Speen; the foot which were there retired to the hedge next the large field between Speen and Newbury; which they made good: at the same time, the right wing of the enemy's horse advanced under the hill of Speen, with one hundred musketeers in the van, and came into the open field, where a good body of the king's horse stood, which

at first received them in some disorder; but the queen's
regiment of horse, commanded by sir John Cansfield,
charged them with so much gallantry, that he routed that
great body; which then fled; and he had the execution of
them near half a mile; wherein most of the musketeers were
slain, and very many of the horse; insomuch that that whole
wing rallied not again that night. The king was at that time
with the prince, and many of the lords, and other his servants, in the middle of that field; and would not, by his
own presence, restrain those horse, which at the first
approach of the enemy were in that disorder, from shame-
fully giving ground. So that if sir John Cansfield had not,
in that article of time, given them that brisk charge, by
which other troops were ready to charge them in the flank,
the king himself had been in very great danger.

At the same time, the left wing of the enemy's horse
advanced towards the north side of the great field; but,
before they got thither, Goring, with the earl of Cleveland's
brigade, charged them so vigorously, that he forced them
back in great confusion over a hedge; and following them,
was charged by another fresh body, which he defeated
likewise, and slew very many of the enemy upon the place;
having not only routed and beaten them on their ground,
but endured the shot of three bodies of their foot in their
pursuit, and in their retreat, with no considerable damage,
save that the earl of Cleveland's horse falling under him, he
was taken prisoner; which was an extraordinary loss. Whilst
this was doing on that side, twelve hundred horse, and three
thousand foot, of those under the earl of Manchester,
advanced with great resolution upon Shaw-house, and the
field adjacent; which quarter was defended by sir Jacob
Astley and colonel George Lisle; and the house, by lieutenant colonel Page. They came singing of psalms; and, at
first, drove forty musketeers from a hedge, who were placed
there to stop them; but they were presently charged by sir
John Brown, with the prince's regiment of horse; who did
good execution upon them, till he saw another body of their
horse ready to charge him, which made him retire to the

foot in Mr Doleman's garden, which flanked that field, and gave fire upon those horse, whereof very many fell; and the horse thereupon wheeling about, sir John Brown fell upon their rear, killed many, and kept that ground all the day; when the reserve of foot, commanded by colonel Thelwell, galled their foot with several vollies, and then fell on them with the but-ends of their muskets, till they had not only beaten them from the hedges, but quite out of the field; leaving two drakes, some colours, and many dead bodies behind them. At this time, a great body of their foot attempted Mr Doleman's house, but were so well entertained by lieutenant colonel Page, that, after they had made their first effort, they were forced to retire in such confusion, that he pursued them from the house with a notable execution, insomuch that they left five hundred dead upon a little spot of ground; and they drew off the two drakes out of the field to the house, the enemy being beaten off, and retired from all that quarter.

It was now night; for which neither party was sorry; and the king, who had been on that side where the enemy only had prevailed, thought that his army had suffered alike in all other places. He saw they were entirely possessed of Speen, and had taken all the ordnance which had been left there; whereby it would be easy for them, before the next morning, to have compassed him round; towards which they might have gone far, if they had found themselves in a condition to have pursued their fortune.

Hereupon, as soon as it was night, his majesty, with the prince, and those lords who had been about him all the day, and his regiment of guards, retired into the fields under Donnington-castle, and resolved to prosecute the resolution that was taken in the morning, when they saw the great advantage the enemy had in numbers, with which he was like to be encompassed, if his forces were beaten from either of the posts. That resolution was, 'to march away in the night towards Wallingford'; and to that purpose, all the carriages and great ordnance had been that morning drawn under Donnington-castle; so he sent orders to all the officers to draw off their men to the same place; and receiving intelligence at that time that prince Rupert was come, or would be that night at Bath, that he might make no stay there, but presently be able to join with his army, his majesty himself, with the prince, and about three hundred horse, made haste thither, and found prince Rupert there, and thence made what haste they could back towards Oxford. The truth is, the king's army was not in so ill a condition, as the king conceived it to have been: that party which were in the field near Speen, kept their ground very resolutely; and although it was a fair moonshine night, the enemy, that was very near them, and much superior in number, thought not fit to assault or disturb them. That part of the enemy that had been so roughly treated at Shaw, having received succour of a strong body of horse, resolved once more to make an attempt upon the foot there; but they were beaten off as before.

INDEX

(Roman numerals in *italics* refer to the maps)